GALWAY
A Sense of Place

About the Author

Roddy Mannion is an architect, originally from County Galway, who has lived and worked in the city, where he has his own practice, for the past 25 years. He is the consultant architect for the New Port of Galway and has prepared an Urban Design Framework for the existing harbour, both of which involved considerable research, study and writing about Galway, which eventually resulted in *Galway: A Sense of Place*.

GALWAY

A SENSE OF PLACE

Roddy Mannion

The Liffey Press

Published by
The Liffey Press Ltd
Raheny Shopping Centre, Second Floor
Raheny, Dublin 5, Ireland
www.theliffeypress.com

A catalogue record of this book is
available from the British Library.

ISBN 978-1-908308-19-1

Printed in Spain by GraphyCems.

CONTENTS

Preface   *ix*
Foreword by Sean O'Laoire   *xvii*

PART ONE: THE EVOLUTION OF THE CITY

Defined by Water   **3**

Galway Bay   5
River Corrib   8
Lough Corrib   11
Lough Atalia   12
Eglington Canal   14
The Harbour Basin   15
Rain   16

Shaped by Foreigners   **17**

The Normans   19
The Anglo-Normans   21
The English   24
The Religious Orders   25
The Americans   27
The Tourists   29

Created in Stone   **31**

Nature of Stone   34
Galway Stone   37
Raw Materials   39
Construction   40
Stone Styles   42

Development of the City   **47**

The Walled Town   48

The Medieval Era   50

Stagnation Period   52

Struggle Back to a City   54

Decline and Slow Recovery   56

Gaelic Settlements   **57**

The Claddagh   58

Menlo Village   59

The Modern Era   **61**

Suburban Galway   64

Shopping and Other Centres   68

Urban Galway   71

PART TWO: GALWAY'S SENSE OF PLACE

Architecture and Buildings   **82**

St. Nicholas' Church   82

Lynch's Castle   83

Spanish Arch   84

Mayoralty House   85

Courthouse   85

National University Ireland Galway   86

Franciscan Church   87

Meyrick Hotel & Railway Station   87

St. Mary's College   88

UCHG Hospital & Nurses Home   88

Galway Cathedral   90

NUIG Arts Block   91

Galway Education Centre   92

Galway–Mayo Institute of Technology   93

Galway City Museum   93

Neighbourhoods   95

Eyre Square   95
Shop Street   96
The Fishmarket   97
The Docks   98
Woodquay   99
Waterside   99
The Claddagh   100
Waterways Area   101
The West   102
Salthill   102
NUI Galway   103

Arts and Culture   106

Druid Theatre Company   108
Galway Arts Festival   109
Macnas   110
Galway Races   111
Galway Maritime Festivals   112
Sporting Galway   113

Other Elements   115

University Life   115
Pubs and Traditional Music   116
Pedestrianisation   118
Street Culture   120
Galwegians of Note   122
Visitors   126
Saturday Market   128
Eyre Square Fountain   130
Lanes and Alleys   131
Quirks and Features   131
Local Shops   134
The Craic   134
City of Commerce   136
Galway Tiger   138

Image and Substance, Myth and Reality   139

PART THREE: LOOKING AHEAD – WHAT KIND OF FUTURE FOR GALWAY?

Ireland and Cities   150

Irish City Planning and Development   154

Sustainability   159

Galway's Particular Characteristics   162
Geography, Access and Entrance   166
Topography and Conduits of the City   168
Water Frontage, Open Space and Village Centres   169
Urban Mindset   170
Galway's Future Growth   172
Traffic and Transport   178
The Historic Sustainable City   187
City Centre and Commercial Suburbs   189

Towards a New Approach   191
Information Gathering   192
Using Existing Resources   193
Urban Design-led City   195

Vision for the Future City   196
The Roofhome City   199
The Seafront Railway City   201
The Riverfront 'Green' City   203
The Cultural City   206
The Tourist City   209
The Home and Neighbourhood   216
City Twinning   218
City Image   219

Summary – A Sense of Place   221
Bibliography   225
Index   227

PREFACE

Welcoming, appealing, vibrant, delightful, historical, arty, traditional, charming, dynamic, cosmopolitan, bohemian, atmospheric, energetic, colourful, bilingual, medieval, buzzing, fun loving, exuberant, party town, ancient and modern, blend of old and new, cultural.

These are some of the words and phrases that are most used to describe Galway City today. In general, guide books and tourist literature, as well as print, broadcast and social media, are positive and complementary towards the city. Galway in recent times has been established as an exciting and seductive city to visit and an attractive and desirable place to live. This book explores the reasons why the city is so addictive and appealing, and studies its image behind the mere labels and popular opinion. It examines the substance of the city and endeavours to reveal its core essence in all its complexities. Crucially, it looks to the future and tries to chart a direction to address the challenges of growth, change and how to maintain its quality of life.

Galway City is home to 75,000 people and receives around two million visitors a year. It is located at the north-western corner of Galway Bay, on the central western coast of Ireland, at the edge of Europe and facing on to the Atlantic Ocean. The city has its origins in medieval times and has enjoyed and endured both a prosperous and impoverished history. It has been a witness to conquest and conflict, political and religious difference, sieges and rebellion, cultural and social changes.

Straddling the banks of the River Corrib, between Lough Corrib and the sea, it is defined by the Clare Hills, sheltered by the Aran Islands, warmed by the Gulf Stream and exposed to the prevailing winds and rain.

Shop fronts in Galway

It remains the third largest city in Ireland, capital city on the west coast and gateway to Connemara, Aran Islands, Corrib County and the Burren. Galway's attraction as a city is centred on its medieval core against the backdrop setting of its extensive waterways, the resort village and scenery of Salthill and its location in a scenic hinterland. Its desirability as a place to live is derived from its natural and urban landscape, its social and cultural attractions, and the range of services, facilities and amenities it offers.

Galway, like any city, is a complex tapestry with its own particular physical, cultural, economic and social layers and meaning. These layers include the natural and built city, born out of a tiny settlement at a strategic river/sea location which continues to grow, each generation grafting on to the previous with their own values, aspirations and attitudes. It includes its inhabitants, a varied mix of people of different backgrounds, origin and purpose, brought together by fate and going about their rhythm of life, routine and rituals. It includes its social and cultural life, a reflection of the residents' choice on how they wish to live and enjoy life, build relationships, form communities and express themselves. It includes its economic activity, which underpins the city's very existence, survival and growth. Finally, it includes the visitors to the city, who come to observe the varied mosaic and become part of the narrative for a while.

A SENSE OF PLACE

Every city has its own unique sense of place. It is how we distinguish between them and how we decide on our preferences. A sense of place is important because our identity is often defined by locality and our desire to belong. The idea of a sense of place is quite appealing, generally understood, but still somewhat elusive. Its elusiveness comes from the unusual combination of two very different and contrasting words, not just in terms of meaning but on how they draw on our two basic human resources – our ability to think and to feel. Thus 'place' is determined by our thinking process and how we visualise a location in a physical, objective and tangible way. 'Sense', however, is shaped by our feeling ability and how we respond to a place, in an instinctive, subliminal and personal way. So while place can be described, rationally and scientifically, in terms of quantity, its sense has to be experienced subjectively and emotionally in terms of quality.

What are the key ingredients in a sense of place? The dominant, visible element is what's known as the cultural place, a mixture of the natural environment, formed by climate and shaped by human activity. The natural landscape is defined by land, both landform and land cover, and at times by water, freshwater or saltwater. Climate is determined by the actions of sun, rain and wind. Human endeavour creates an imprint on the natural environment which can be formed and reformed over time. These three processes are the basic building blocks of a sense of place, which creates the current canvas on which landscape and climate continues to act and human forces continue to impact.

In a place with a significant settlement, human activity takes on a greater importance and has a more proportional impact on its sense of place. This importance takes the form of the built settlement, formed and expanded over time and reflecting each era's life, values and sense of purpose. Human presence brings a further dimension to place. Human occupation animates, enriches and gives meaning to place. And whether

The Claddagh and Long Walk, Galway City

the endeavour involves inhabiting and participating in place or visiting and observing it, both contribute to the cultural imprint. Participating in a place involves engaging in relationships, centred on community which creates its larger general society. Visiting a place consists of observing that society and its activities. Accordingly, a sense of place will be coloured by whether it is a permanent or transitory experience. Economics can quickly alter a sense of place, depending on its level of prosperity or impoverishment. The passage of time will also shape a sense of place, both in terms of the place itself, but also crucially in terms of the viewer. Response to place will also be influenced by various diverse factors such as age, background, attitude and values.

In summary, a sense of place is the unique, physical, climatic, cultural, social and economic composition of a certain location, which we respond to in an equally unique way. It is a combination of the visible and the hidden, the conscious and the unconscious, the sensory and the spiritual. In essence, it is the body and soul of a place.

ON A PERSONAL NOTE . . .

Born and raised in the crossroads village of Moylough, twenty-five miles away in north east County Galway, my earliest recollection of Galway was of ritual excursions to the city. My first memory as a young child is sitting in a car at the Waterside area of the city and being aware of the sound and force of the Lough Corrib weir waters while my father, a builder, visited an architect's office – an office I subsequently spent a summer working in nearly twenty years later. Following my father's death, my mother, who took over the business, continued the routine of going to Galway on a fairly regular basis. I recall being brought to the opening of Galway Cathedral, of which the fireworks display over the river is my clearest recollection. As an older child, I remember the tradition of going to Ryan's shop for clothes, Brennan's for shoes, Naughton's for sports gear, O'Gorman's for books, Glynn's for school items, but more importantly, shopping in Woolworth's for sweets and Lydon's for chocolate and cream buns.

Hot summer days always involved going to Salthill to swim and to picnic, making sandcastles to earn a whipped ice cream cone and where I was also aware that my grandmother always spent her annual week's holiday there. Watching the salmon over the Salmon Weir Bridge was always a fascinating ritual, and as part of the encouragement of Irish and drama in secondary school visits to the Taibhdhearc Theatre was an occasional event. During secondary school and college holiday periods and working in the family business, my visits to Galway centred on getting building materials in the various providers such as McDonagh's, Higgins's, Hynes's, Corbett's and Coen's. As an architectural student in Dublin there was an annual pilgrimage for Galway University Rag week, culminating in the once-off pilgrimage for Pope John Paul's visit in my final student year in 1979. My subsequent two years' work experience in

Dublin and seven years in Limerick was punctuated by weekend visits to Galway to enjoy the social and cultural life in Salthill and the city centre, particularly in High Street and Quay Street, and to observe the inventiveness of Druid and the spectacle of Macnas.

I started to work in Galway in 1988, where my first job was as project, rather than design, architect on the Eyre Square Shopping Centre, ironically the site of my college final year design thesis, which was more of a revealing than rewarding experience and prompted me to start my own practice in 1990. This coincided with the biggest building programme the city had seen in over 200 years and I was fortunate to be involved in many of the urban renewal projects, particularly in the city centre, for the subsequent fifteen years. During that time and despite its cosmopolitan and bohemian reputation, I found Galway quite traditional and even conservative at its core. In the early years, I lived over my work in the city centre, but after getting married and becoming a father, subsequently moved to the suburbs of the city, where my experience of its transitory population later prompted me to move just outside the city boundary, which is destined to become part of the city in the coming years. I still continue to work in the city centre and now have ritual visits with my own family into town. Recently, I was involved as consultant architect on the New Port for Galway and preparing the Urban Design Framework document for the existing harbour, a body of work which involved a considerable amount of research, study and writing about the harbour and general city, which attracted me to the idea of expanding it to a more extensive and comprehensive book on the city and its sense of place. I was also curious about a recent newspaper feature on the city, where a local businessman expressed uncertainty as to why the city was so popular, but also fearful that its popularity might be fragile.

My experience of the city, therefore, is one of a visitor and then resident, of a worker and then business owner, of an observer and then participant, so this book is a result of all my personal and professional experience, knowledge, observations of the city from a young age. The book is divided into three parts, 'The Evolution of the City', 'Galway's Sense of Place' and 'Looking Ahead – What Kind of Future for Galway?' Part One looks at the natural, historical and physical evolution of the city based on a fine body of research and history contained in numerous publications on the city, distilled and interpreted to illustrate its sense of place. Part Two looks at the architecture, neighbourhoods, cultural institutions and unique features that make up Galway's sense of place. Finally, Part Three examines the next fifty years and beyond to look at the challenges facing Galway's development and offers some suggestions on how it might evolve. Collectively, the three parts are about learning from the past and defining the present in order to anticipate and shape the future. At all times, an understanding and appreciation of Galway's sense of place remains at the core of the book and the primary purpose for writing it. I hope you enjoy reading it as much as I enjoyed writing it.

Acknowledgements

I would like to acknowledge and thank the following for their help and assistance: David Givens from The Liffey Press; Josephine Vahey and the staff of Galway City Library; Joe O'Neill, Caroline Feelan and Sinead Johnson in Galway City Council; Cait Curran from Galway's Saturday Market.

I would like to thank the following for supplying various photographs and images: Mike Shaughnessy (pages 4/5, 30, 107, 110, 112, 114, 220); Failte Ireland (pages xii, 61, 121, 130, 145, 146); Michael Bourke (pages 10, 11, 78, 83, 151, 205); Gavin Duffy (pages 157, 192, 196); Galway Arts Festival (pages 95, 109); Greg Power, NUIG (pages 105 (Nos. 5, 15)); Stephen Power (page 117); Galway Race Committee (page 111); Michael Cadden, OPW (page 20); Reg Gordan (page 123 (Ollie Jennings)); individual 'Galwegians' for their respective portraits (pages 123).

I am very thankful to Derek Concannon who patiently prepared all the drawings and maps.

I am very grateful to Sean O'Laoire for his foreword and for being an inspiration over the years.

Roddy Mannion
May 2012
Galway City

Dedication

I would like to dedicate this book to my wife Joan
and children Julie, Rory and David.

FOREWORD

SEAN O'LAOIRE

It was 1960. There was no television (or sex) in Ireland. It was a mono-tonic place. Galway was a pit-stop on a rite of passage to An Gaeltacht – a place uncontaminated by alien oppressors. Our minder, a muscular Christian Brother, did concede that Galway was at very least more 'Irish', and therefore more pure, than the post-colonial cesspit – Dublin – I was unfortunate enough to have been born into. But still not a place in which to risk the fragile morals or hormones of an adolescent. A seminal mo-ment, which I now believe spawned a life-long interest in cities, and a fascination and deep affection for Galway – a place which has tangentially touched me, and I have tangentially touched, personally and profession-ally, over a period of forty years.

I am deeply honoured therefore to write this foreword to Roddy Man-nion's book. I have known Roddy as a student, a professional colleague, and latterly as a collaborator. This book is not a labour of love. It is a true love story – a story of profound love for a place which he cherishes, as do so many people in Ireland, and throughout the world. A love that, while unconditional, is yet strong enough to acknowledge warts and weakness-es and, critically, a love that inspires a passion, in these bleak times, to postulate a vision for its future.

James Joyce, who was undoubtedly a tribal descendant of Galway, noted that, 'if Ireland is to become a new Ireland, she must first become European'. Seeing a city on the edge of Europe as 'European' would have challenged my Christian Brother minder. But in my imagined Galway, in the grey Ireland of my youth, it didn't matter whether it was verifiable that Christopher Columbus visited the city, or that somewhere in the Caribbean are the descendants of a young Galwayman he reputedly took to the New World with him. Nor did it matter that the lighthouse portrayed in Hardiman's map of medieval Galway, rivalling that of Ancient Alexandria, was perhaps a fantasy. What did matter in my imagined Galway was its colour and its layered connections with magical and exotic places like Bordeaux, Nantes, Lisbon, Porto, Seville, the West Indies and Newfoundland. My then grey crumbling Dublin exported cattle and people on the hoof to Liverpool.

The fates converged fully ten years later to place me as a naïve foot soldier surveying every field on the periphery of a city, centred on its magic tissue of medieval streets, and only lightly touched by neo-classicism and later layers of European urbanisation.

That event heralded the greatest epoch of expansion of the city in 1,000 years – compressed into forty years. Suburban Galway, with its amorphous disconnected accretions, mirrors suburban Ireland in embodying the Irish paradox. Seventy per cent of Irish people live in some form of diluted urbanity, while nostalgically aspiring to an elusive rural idyll at the expense of a sustainable and rich urban culture.

Despite this, it is the strength of the mental map and lived experience of the medieval core of the city that still defines Galway today – a archetypal European post-medieval urban settlement, whose genius loci or sense of place derives from the symphonic confluence of majestic ocean, wild river, saline marsh and western light, with dense urban grain and rugged textures – and with its people, its accents, its music its voices – a place apart.

Today, it is the children of the exotic places that Galway once traded with that re-connect the periphery of Europe to its continental land mass and beyond.

The fates again conspired to place me on a wild and windy night on the turbulent Corribs banks in the mid-1980s, to witness Els Comediants from Catalonia disembark to invade the city, and set it on fire, metaphorically and physically – thereby reconnecting with Iberia and spawning Macnas – now a synonym internationally for Galway's propensity for exuberance and celebration, 'The Playground of the Western World'.

James Joyce, with *Ulysses*, gifted to humanity, in perpetuity, the freedom of the City of his imagined Metropolis Dublin, of the 16th June 1904. But he had an Achilles Heel. He lost his heart to a Galway Girl. In a country and culture still ambivalent and sometimes collusively permissive in its engagement with cities, this gift is supremely ironic.

Equally ironic is the fact that it is the shadow of Galway, not Dublin, that hangs spectre-like over possibly the greatest short story in world literature: 'The Dead', the cornerstone of Joyce's *Dubliners* collection.

Across 'the dark mutinous Shannon waves', not in a 'lonely churchyard on a hill' but in Rahoon cemetery, lay the remains of Nora Barnacle's young love, Michael Bodkin, portrayed as Michael Furey in 'The Dead' – a memory that consumed Joyce. His alter ego in the story, Gabriel Conroy, in the famous last paragraph, recognised that 'the time has come for him to set out on his journey west'.

Roddy Mannion's gift has no pretence to be a Galwegian *Ulysses*. Rather it is an invitation to you, Dear Reader, to set out on the journey west, and share his sense of his Galway – a place that must, and will in time, resist bastion-like the global spread of urban mono-culture.

Share your place with his. Carry this book in your car. Place it by your bed. Take it with you when you walk. Discuss it and start rows – most of all cherish it and the unique place on the edge of the western world it interrogates and celebrates – and imagine – *Gaillimh Abu*.

Beir Bua is Beannacht.

Sean O'Laoire is an architect and former President of the Royal Institute of Architects of Ireland.

Illustration from Hardiman's History of Galway, *1820*

Part One

THE EVOLUTION OF THE CITY

A grey town in a country bare, the leaden seas between,
When the light falls on the hills of Clare
And shows their valleys green.
Take in my heart your place again
Between your lake and sea
Oh city of the watery plain, that means so much to me.

Your cut stone houses row on row
Your streams too deep to sing
Whose waters shine with green as though
They had dissolved the Spring.

Your streets that still bring into view the harbour and its spars.
The chimneys with their turf smoke blue that never hides the stars.
Take in my heart your place again between your lake and sea
Like crimson roses in grey walls your memories to me.
It is not very long since you, for memory is long,
Saw her I owe my being to, and heart that takes to song,
Walk with a row of laughing girls from Salthill to Eyre Square
Light from the water on their curls that never lit more fair.
Take in my heart your place again between your lake and sea,
Like crimson roses in grey walls your memories to me.

Again may come your glorious days, your ships come back to port,
And to your city's shining ways the Spanish girls resort.
And e'er the tidal water falls, your ships put out to sea
Like crimson roses in grey walls your memories to me.
Take in my heart your place again between your lake and sea

Oh, city of the watery plain, that means so much to me.

– 'Galway', Oliver St. John Gogarty

INTRODUCTION

Despite all the words written about Galway City, including its frequent source of inspiration in popular culture, it is Oliver St. John Gogarty's poem, written in the last century, that best captures its sense of place – its natural setting overlaid with a mix of built, cultural and social layers. Like all cities, Galway's sense of place is primarily determined by its natural environment and the overlying mosaic of human activity since its birth. The creation of Galway as we see it today was a complex process involving almost 800 years of growth and change. Trying to classify the main elements that contribute to its unique, intricate weave is not easy. However, as a starting point, and particularly in Ireland, the clues can often be found in the origin of the name, or in Galway's case, the uncertainty as to the origin of the name.

The source of the placename Galway (*Gaillimh* in Irish) has been a matter of debate for centuries, with many suggestions based on fact and folklore. One explanation was that it derived from *gall* and *aimh*, two words that seem to denote a stony river. However, it is also known that amongst the Gaelic Irish, foreigners were called the *na gall,* hence the suggestion that Gaillimh was the place of the foreigners. Others believe that it derives from *galmhaith,* meaning stony barren ground as *gall* was also an old Irish name for stone. Finally, myth and legend suggest that it derives from a mythological princess called Galvia, said to have drowned in its waters.

The theme of water, foreigner and stone emerge from the possible origin of its placename, and each has a sense of truth in describing the place. Ironically, therefore, it is the combined ambiguity of its placename source that best captures the spirit and essence of the place, for Galway, perhaps more than any city in Ireland, is a city defined by water, created in stone and shaped by foreigners. These are the themes that reveal its natural landscape, its built heritage and the humans who have populated it. They are also the themes that we can explore to give us the best understanding, and the best description, of Galway's unique sense of place.

Defined by Water

I know a town tormented by the sea
And there time goes slow
That the people see it flow
And watch it drowsily

– M.D. O'Neill, 1929

The presence of water, both saline and fresh is, above all of Galway's features, the dominant informant of its natural sense of place. Water is ever present in the city and in many ways defines it, both in terms of its origin, layout and growth, but also its quantity, variety and quality. Galway is the only city in Ireland that is home to five generic waterbodies and watercourses, namely, river, lake, sea, canal and harbour basin – the former three being natural features and the latter two man-made. Galway owes its birth to water, founded as it was at a strategic frontier fort where the River Corrib flows into the sea. It also owes its subsequent growth to water, with the bay providing the conduit for international sea trade and sea fishing, and the lake and river for internal trade. Lough Corrib,

the largest lake in Ireland, forms the northern boundary of the city. It flows into the fast flowing but gentle serpentine of the River Corrib, which at less than 5 kilometres long is the shortest river in Europe and divides the city in two. The Eglington Canal, and its venous system of channels, snakes through its west inner city streetscape, while Lough Atalia, the salt water lake, caresses the east inner city and suburbs. The harbour basin brings the sea into the bosom of the city, as historically the oldest part of the medieval city centre clustered next to its harbour and quays. Finally, all waters discharge into the wide tidal sweep of Galway Bay, immortalised in song and guarded at its entrance by the three Aran Islands.

The variety of water types in the city is matched with a corresponding variety in the nature of the waters. The relative calm of Lough Corrib contrasts sharply with the powerful surge that is River Corrib, as the relatively narrow river needs to discharge quickly into the sea to accommodate the surplus waters of the large lake. The canal flows with a gentle rhythm, whilst Lough Atalia, though tidal, is sheltered from the sea breezes due to the surrounding townscape. The bay provides the most extremes, ranging from gentle lapping and ebbing tides to wind-lashed waves which flood parts of the city at high tide.

Archaeological evidence shows that even before the founding of the city the area was occupied up to 5,000 years prior to its construction, as historically people have always chosen to live beside rivers, lakes and the sea, as they provided a source of food and water as well as the means to travel from one location to another. Consequently, water in all its various forms in Galway has been the main natural theme and common denominator in the city since Mesolithic times.

Galway Bay

You may sit and watch the turf fire in the Claddagh
And watch the sun go down on Galway Bay
– 'Galway Bay', Bing Crosby, 1950

If you could make chains with the morning dew
The world would be like Galway Bay
– 'The Luck of the Irish', John Lennon, 1965

And the NYPD choir were singing Galway Bay
And the bells were ringing out on Christmas Day
– 'Fairytale of New York', Shane McGowan, 1980

Any waterbody that unites and inspires such diverse personalities as Bing Crosby, John Lennon and Shane McGowan must have an unusual attraction.

Galway Bay is a large sea inlet approximately 50 kilometres long and between 10 and 30 kilometres wide, bounded by Galway to the north, the Burren of County Clare to the south with the three Aran Islands across its entrance. In the old Irish annals it was known as Lough Lurgan, in the belief that it was once a lake which subsequently became part of the ocean when the sea flooded over its exposed entrance, leaving the Aran Islands standing. Whatever about the legend, the scenic attraction of Galway Bay has been acknowledged and appreciated for almost 200 years. That attraction curiously enough owes more to Clare than Galway for it is the bare, karastic limestone hills of Clare that gives the bay its scenic backdrop and most defining features, which is ironically missing from the Clare side of the bay – a case of Clare providing the scenery, but Galway controlling the brand name. For Galway city, the bay has traditionally provided it with its main tourist attraction and trademark. That tourist appeal was first developed in the tourist resort of Salthill in the middle of the nineteenth century, but reached brand status when Bing Crosby immortalised it in song in 1950. The song, written by Englishman Arthur Colahan who studied in University College Galway, was of course overly romantic and nostalgic, tapping into the sentimental view of Irish American and Irish English emigrants, but the Irish Tourist Board or Galway never complained.

Prior to that, Galway Bay had been the source of sustenance, trading, invasion and emigration for the city. Its primary function since ancient times was providing a wide range of fish for consumption, including herring, mackerel, cod and ray. Its fishing past was best embodied in the Galway Hooker, a distinctive brown fishing boat which operated out of the Claddagh fishing village. Hardiman, in his *History of Galway* (1820), described the sight of 500 fishing boats from the Claddagh:

> *The beauty of the sight is incredible and when viewed from one of the heights above the town is perhaps one of the most satisfying that can well be imagined.*

Galway Bay

However, with fishing also came fear, and with sustenance also came sadness. The bay has experienced a history of fishing tragedies and loss of life over the years, as represented in the Claddagh monument to lost fishermen and in Synge's immortal lines of the mother, from 'Riders to the Sea': 'they're all gone now, there's nothing more the sea can do to me'. Along with fishing, shipping was its trading relation, with the bay providing the highway for all shipping routes to distant ports in Europe and the Americas. In the post-famine years, the ships also included the cruise ships serving the new developing tourist market in Victorian Ireland. Their welcoming sight was offset by the discomforting scene of emigrants utilising the cruise ships on their return leg to America.

The threat of invasion which the bay presented was not just confined to the Norse raiders of the ninth century. In the Elizabethan era of the sixteenth century, the bay and city were regarded as prime strategic targets for a Spanish invasion of the British Empire, through Galway, as evidenced by the ill-fated Spanish Armada which floundered in the bay in 1588, leading to the execution of 300 Spanish sailors by British forces in the city and subsequently buried in Forthill Cemetery.

Today, however, it is Salthill, the beach resort area of the city, that encapsulates the significance of Galway Bay to the city. The scenery and bathing attractions of Salthill were first exploited by the coming of the railway to the city in 1851. By 1879, it was responsible for Galway's first public transport system, a horse-drawn tramway which linked the resort to the railway station. During those Victorian times, the sea bathing tradition was combined with the health restorative benefits of the spa and seaweed baths. During the twentieth century it developed into the distinctive Irish seaside resort type adjoining a large city, such as Dublin/Bray, Cork/Cobh, Limerick/Kilkee, attracting primarily rural farming families after the harvesting was done. With the explosion of tourism in the late 1950s, it changed again into a holiday, social and amusement location of beaches, seaside kiosks, hotels, ballrooms and amusement arcades, against the backdrop of the salty, windy air and smell of seaweed, remnants of which still exist today. However, its modern feel now, physically connected to the city, is one of a village centre serving the local, western, coastal side of the city and the very popular Galway pastime of 'walking the prom' and tradition of 'kicking the wall' near Blackrock diving board. Given the climate, the indoor facilities of Lesiureland and the Atlantaquarium offer a welcome alternative to the outdoor attractions of prom, beach, park, playground and fairground.

And yes, it is possible on a clear evening, to watch the sun go down on Galway Bay – if you can get a clear evening.

River Corrib

The waters of Lough Corrib,
which permeates under the bridges of the town
go rushing and roaring to the sea
with a noise and eagerness only known in Galway
– W.M. Thackeray, 1842

Salmon in the Corrib
Gently swaying
And the water combed out
Over the weir
– 'Galway', Louis McNeice, 1939

In the casual and laid back atmosphere that is Galway, the River Corrib is arguably the most hurried thing in the city. The fast-flowing river needs to be in a hurry. Taking all the surplus waters from Lough Corrib and Lough Mask to the sea in an area of high rainfall and through a narrow channel requires speed and mobility. It explains why Galway is said to be originally known as *Baile na Sruthain* – the town of the streams – because the waters flowed through the town in high winter floods. Today, however, the river is regulated by a weir at the entrance to the city, constructed in 1852 and reconstructed in 1961, to allow a maximum discharge of 1,000 cubic feet of water per second through the city. The streams are now confined to a series of five other waterways, each side of the river, which leaves the main river as it enters the city and rejoins it before the estuary enters the bay.

Besides its physical presence, the river has mythological, historical, ecological, economic and recreational meaning for the city. The mythological figure of Galvia, daughter of King Breasal from the legendary island of Hy Brazil, was reportedly drowned in the waters and gave the river

River Corrib

its original name. The place where she was drowned was even included in the famous 1651 pictorial map of the city. The bed of the river carries the secrets of the city, gradually revealing itself in the many prehistoric artefacts recovered by divers which indicate the presence of human activity in the city as far back as 6,000 BC. Historically, the river acted as a conduit for transport, as a highway for navigation bringing goods to and from the city. It was also the corridor through which the Christian Monastic wealth on and around Lough Corrib attracted the predatory instincts of Viking raiders during the ninth century. Its economic value was recognised and exploited from ancient times, through fishing its generous supply of salmon, and during the nineteenth century through its power, fuelling over eighty mills of various types. Its ecological and even social amenity importance manifested itself in the sight of shoals of wild salmon visible from the Salmon Weir Bridge, as they rested on their annual summer run before leaping and completing their journey back to their spawning ground in Lough Corrib. Today, the amenity of the river is

Salmon weir area

amplified with a sequence of riverside walks and the continuing and very popular recreational tradition of rowing, with five different rowing clubs operating from above the weir of the river.

For the city today, the River Corrib and its bridges represent the symbolic dividing, meeting, crossing and transition between the east and west of not only both sides of the city, but both sides of the county. Its symbolism is defined by the fact that its ford crossing in the eleventh century became the reason for the subsequent tribal power struggle and eventual birthplace of the city itself.

Lough Corrib

Lough Corrib is the source of life for Galway City. Besides supplying the river's rushing waters, it also supplies the city's drinking water, a fact generally unknown, until supply was interrupted in 2007, when pollution in the lake caused contamination of the supply. Consequently, the health and well being of the city is dependent on the health and well being of the lake.

While the lake forms the northern boundary of the city, it does not feature prominently in its identity, mainly due to being removed from the main urban and suburban areas and the poor accessibility to, and visibility of, its waters. This is likely to change with the development of the new outer city bypass, which will bring the lake more into the con-

Lough Corrib

11

sciousness of the city. Despite its removed status, it is seen as an extension of the River Corrib to whom it supplies its surplus water, and consequently has a direct if somewhat second-hand relationship with the city.

The lake itself is the largest in the Republic of Ireland, covering an area of 180 square kilometres and at its maximum measures 45 kilometres long and 21 kilometres wide. It is visually a quite varied lake, containing an estimated 145 islands and a sequence of shallows, deeps, bays, inlets and peninsulas against a surrounding backdrop of mountains, hills and plains. An attempt to connect the lake by canal to the adjacent Lough Mask in County Mayo in the post-famine years was finally unsuccessful after five years of work, due to the underlying limestone bedrock geology of the area. It is a lake rich in history, where its islands and perimeter banks, housed thirty-one early Christian Monastic sites. Its most famous island, Inchigoill, or 'Island of the Devout Stranger', has two early Christian churches, whilst St. Brendan the Navigator founded a monastery in Inchiquin island in the sixth century and died nearby at Annaghdown. Its most famous recent visitor was William Wilde, father of Oscar Wilde, who owned a home on its shoreline and who wrote extensively about the lake in the nineteenth century.

Today, besides its recognised tourist attraction, Lough Corrib is more famous for its fishing, attracting more anglers than any other fishery in Ireland, mainly for trout and salmon and, particularly, the annual Corrib mayfly in the last two weeks of May. Galway City's boundary interface with the lake at Menlo is symbolically signposted by a partially collapsed megalithic tomb, in the form of a portal dolman, dating back to 3,000 BC, which is the oldest known structure in the city.

Lough Atalia

If Lough Atalia was located in an inland city it would be regarded as an amenity jewel to be utilised and enjoyed by the city. However, because Galway has such an extensive network and stock of waterways and waterbodies, it remains a passive visual amenity only, surprisingly unexploited for such a calm and sheltered city lake and forming an attractive lakeside road entrance to the city from the east. It is from the railway line, however, at the bridge over the Lough Atalia Channel, which provides the

Lough Atalia

most spectacular view, creating the most dramatic railway entrance to any city in Ireland.

The lake itself, Lough Atalia or Salt Lake, is a small enclosed tidal lake, 0.5 square kilometres in area with a narrow channel connecting it to the inner bay and river estuary. It was at the periphery of the city until the 1970s, but is now enclosed by the eastern inner city and inner suburbs. The Galway Bay Sailing Club has its origins in Lough Atalia where early members sailed on small craft twice weekly in the late 1960s before moving to their present location in Rinville in the mid-1970s. The lake was the site of three holy wells – of which only one survives – dedicated to St. Augustine after the Augustine Friary which was founded nearby in 1508. The holy well was regarded as having curative powers and was a place of pilgrimage on the 28th of August each year. Today the well is represented by a high cross which is visible at high tide but reveals the sacred site at low tide.

Eglinton Canal

Eglinton Canal

The Eglinton Canal can be seen as either a monument to folly or to enterprise, depending on which side of the canal bank one stands. It was part of a network of canal systems in Ireland during the middle of the nineteenth century, most of which were commercially unviable. The canal is 1,200 metres long and was designed to open up Connemara and Mayo to trade with Galway and the outside world by facilitating the movement of goods connecting Lough Corrib to the sea. It was also designed to regulate the water supply to the large number of mills and other industries utilising water power at that time.

Constructed during the famine years where it provided much needed labour, it was opened in 1842 by Lord Eglinton, the Lord Lieutenant of Ireland. It incorporated five swivel bridges, lock gates and the Claddagh Basin in its design, and while it enjoyed initial success, its growth was constrained by improvements in the road network and the opening of the Dublin/Galway railway line around the same time. The subsequent opening of the Galway/Clifton line in 1895 sealed its fate, and though it continued in use until 1954, it was no longer a commercial enterprise. The swing bridges were replaced with fixed concrete bridges around that time and the canal ceased to be navigable. Today it provides a sinuous water amenity for the west inner city and a calming presence in an often energetic city.

The Harbour Basin

The harbour basin is Galway's most visible connection to the outside world with ships arriving and departing to other world port cities. Like Eyre Square, it is an urban space in its own right, where the grass and plaza of the square are replaced by the controlled waters of the harbour. The current harbour was constructed in 1842 during a phase of major infrastructural projects taking part around the city at the time. The original design for the basin was by Alexander Nimmo, the famous Scottish engineer, and following his death was completed by H. Kilkelly. The harbour

The harbour basin

had gradually evolved over hundreds of years since its first location close to the Spanish Arch in the fourteenth century, and the new harbour was to provide deeper waters and a sheltered dock to cater for continually increasing ship sizes. During the twentieth century the basin developed into a combined commercial and recreational port and is the most adjacent harbour in Ireland to the main shopping and business district. Its proximity to the medieval city echoes that of previous harbour incarnations and enjoys high visibility on the main east-west route through the city.

The harbour has an enclosed, intimate and sheltered horseshoe form, which, combined with the amenity value of its waters, provides a seductive urban setting. The fact that the city has extended and enveloped the harbour in recent years has added to its sense of urban enclosure. With the Eglinton Canal it is one of only two man-made waterbodies in the city and a valuable amenity as the city continues to grow. A notable new feature of the harbour basin in recent years is the increasing level of maritime events it is hosting, such as the Volvo Ocean Race, which highlights its capacity to cater for the cultural and social life of the city as well as the shipping industry.

Rain

> *And the rain comes lashin',*
> *Splish splashin',*
> *Down the town.*
> *In a Galway fashion*
> – 'Streets of Galway', Padraig Stevens

Despite its large stock of water, there are parts of the city where it is possible to be removed from its attraction and where its waterways are not visible. However, the leaden skies overhead is a reminder that water from above is about to compensate for that loss. It is said that Galway rain is the reason why its pubs are so enticing or why the streets are a riot of colour, as if there is a repressed need to challenge the elements for their gift of dark, grey clouds and a surplus of rain. Perversely, the variety of colour on offer mirrors the variety of rain on offer. Similarly, the range of the city's surface water matches the range of overhead water.

In Galway, at any given time or season, there is a possibility of vertical rain, diagonal rain or horizontal rain. Alternatively, one can endure a soft mist, a heavy drizzle or a torrential downpour. In addition, there is wind-driven rain, sun-borne rain or gale-forced rain. The final possibility is intermittent rain, persistent rain or just ordinary squally showers. As confirmation of this unfortunate fact, the most common phrase used in Irish weather forecasting, originating in the Dublin Met office, is 'rain spreading from the west', as if Galway was dumping some contagion on Dublin and the Pale as a response to all the perceived humiliations of history. It is significant that the novel that best captures the atmosphere of Galway, by local writer Walter Macken, was titled *Rain on the Wind*. Yes, Galway is a city defined by water – both on the ground and from above.

SHAPED BY FOREIGNERS

> *'Neither O ne Mac should strutte ne swagger through the streets of Galway'* – Medieval Galway Edict

> *The merchants are rich and great adventurers at sea. Their commonality is comprised of the descendants of the ancient England founders of the town and rarely admit any new English to have freedom or education among them and never any of the Irish.*
> – St. Oliver St. John, 1601

The human story of Galway City from its birth in the thirteenth century to the early part of the twentieth century, and again up to the start of the twenty-first century, is one of foreigners of various origins, background and traits. The area was conquered, the city founded and successively occupied by foreigners up to Irish independence in 1922. Foreigners created the historic city as we know it today, developed its political, commercial, cultural and social order for almost 700 years and, even with the creation of the new free state, continued to impact and influence the city in a new guise. Depending on the truth or time period of the name Galway, meaning city of foreigners, it was unlikely to have been a term of endearment or admiration. For the native Irish, the description would have carried a certain tone of disdain but also awe. In

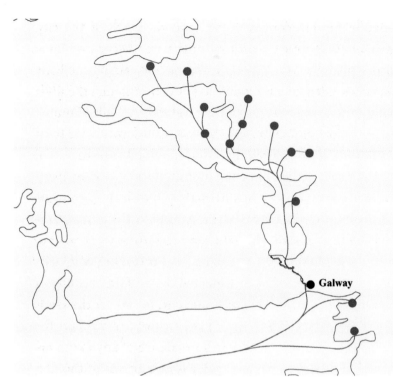

Ninth century Viking raids around Galway

the early development of the city, the foreign founding fathers excluded the local Gaelic Irish. The creation of the walled city defined and cemented the city of 'foreigners', and where ironically the Irish themselves became 'foreigners' within the walls. Gradually, however, the concept of an isolated royalist or loyalist enclave in a Gaelic hinterland became commercially untenable, and the walls and barriers eventually fell victim to commerce between both societies. In addition, the interconnection and crossover between both cultures created the notion of the foreigners becoming more Irish than the Irish themselves and, while greatly exaggerated, certainly changed both cultural traditions and there developed a Hiberno–Anglo–Norman hybrid society. Consequently, and ironically, by the time of Irish independence the term 'foreigner' had lost most of its initial sting, but the exposure of Galway to foreign influences over centuries, both political and trade, helped the city remain open to a new form and era of foreigners in the second half of the twentieth century, this time invited and welcomed.

The influence of foreign conquest preceded the birth of the city. There is evidence of Mesolithic occupation in the area as early as 6,000 BC. There is also evidence of the Vikings invading and raiding the Early Christian monastery settlements around Lough Corrib through the River Corrib route. Unlike most of the main cities of Ireland, including Dublin, Wexford, Waterford, Cork and Limerick, the Vikings did not form a town here, possibly because of their preference for sheltered, inletted, tidal estuaries with a fertile hinterland, in contrast to Galway's more exposed climate, barren lands and possibly hostile natives. Consequently, while Ireland was a late comer to the urban tradition, due to the Roman Empire never extending to these shores, Galway was a further late comer to forming a city. History has recorded that in 1124, the future city originally contained a Gaelic castle, a timber fort erected at the ford crossing of the river by Turlough O'Connor, King of Connacht, to protect the lands controlled by his allies, the O'Hallorans to the east of the city and the O'Flahertys to the west. However, there is no evidence of any major urban settlement being established there, prior to the arrival of the first foreigners in 1232. Whilst we have classified the foreigners into distinct groupings, this is more for clarity and convenience purposes. In reality, none of the non-Irish groupings were a coherent category, nor were they particular to a certain era. History tends to be a lot more fluid and messy than its recording. However, the following will give a flavour of the dominant foreign influences on the physical, cultural, economic and social fortunes of the city which contributed to its sense of place.

The Normans

The founders of the city and its first settlers were the Norman de Burgo family who came to Ireland in the wake of the Anglo/Norman invasion of 1185. Led by Richard de Burgo, they established a castle in 1232 replacing the existing fort settlement of Turlough O'Connor. The de Burgo manorial seat was in Loughrea in east Galway and they used Galway as a location to set up a trading centre, which was developed by their immediate followers into a fortified town. Because of their origins, the language of law, literature, commerce and general society in the new town was Norman/French until the beginning of the fifteenth century, when English

Excavated Red Earl Hall in Druid Lane

became the dominant language. (It is interesting to note that Normandy in France derives its name from Northman or Norseman (Vikings) who invaded and settled there in the ninth century, which indicates that while Galway was not occupied by the early Vikings, it was founded by their later descendents.)

Richard de Burgo replaced the de Burgo castle with a hall, known as the Hall of the Red Earl, in 1271, the foundations of which were uncovered in 1997. Around this time the tenants in the town were granted a charter to tax all trading goods which funded the walled enclosure. The de Burgos continued to maintain a tight control on the affairs of the town, but gradually their descendants became Gaelicised and the name de Burgo was adapted to the later Anglicised name Burke. They lost partial lordship in 1395 when Richard II granted a new charter to the town which changed its status to a royal borough and thus technically under his control. As the town grew in prosperity, they effectively relinquished all power and authority when Richard III elevated the town to one of self-governance with the granting of a charter in 1484, allowing citizens to elect their own mayor and corporation. Despite subsequent power struggles, the de Burgos of Loughrea, and their later descendants the Burkes of Clanrichard, were effectively excluded from the affairs of the town from that date.

The Anglo-Normans

The Anglo-Normans were the immediate and subsequent followers of the Norman de Burgo family and were effectively the founding families of Galway City. The original settlers established themselves as merchants, and as trade grew were joined by others, mainly of Anglo-Norman origin, who had settled within County Galway. The families prospered through trade with the Gaelic hinterland, Continental Europe and later the Americas. They established strong trading links from the port of Galway to England, Spain, France, Italy and Portugal. With the granting of a royal chapter in 1484, they gained, in both church and state affairs, a degree of independence which was unique. Isolated from Dublin, the centre of English authority in Ireland (there were no bridge crossings at Athlone or Ballinasloe at the time), the wealthy merchant families were able to develop a city state and dominate the political, commercial and social life of the city. They commissioned public and religious buildings and built large elaborate houses for themselves within the fortified town, two of which, Lynch's Castle and Blake's Tower, still survive today. They adopted coats of arms often without heraldic authority which were ostentatiously displayed on their houses.

The most prominent merchant family were the Lynches, whose members held the office of mayor eighty-four times during the medieval period. Whilst they shared trade and the same Catholic religion as the native Irish, they were seen as occupying an English-speaking enclave and loyalty within a Gaelic hinterland. The merchant families lost much of their power in Galway with the Cromwellian siege and occupation in 1652, and it was around this time that the title 'Tribes of Galway' was coined, either as a derogatory rebuke from Cromwell's forces or a self-proclaimed

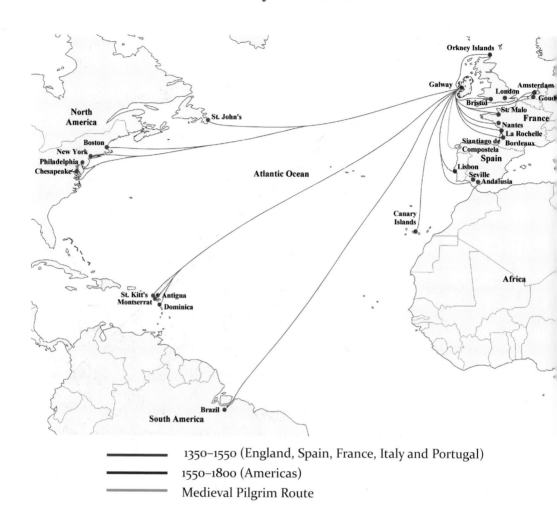

———————	1350–1550 (England, Spain, France, Italy and Portugal)
———————	1550–1800 (Americas)
———————	Medieval Pilgrim Route

Atlantic shipping routes from Galway Port (1350–1800)

mark of pride and defiance by the descendants of the original families. In all there were fourteen recognised tribes, of which two, the Kirwans and D'Arcys, were of Irish origin. After the siege, many of the merchants lost their prosperity and were ordered from the town. Some of them emigrated where they set up new enterprises, such as the Blakes who established a successful tobacco business in the West Indies. Others later returned with the relaxation of the new Protestant order, many of whom resorted to smuggling because of increased taxation. During the three centuries of their power, the merchant families were consistently confronted with the conflicting dilemma of their unique position. Amongst themselves

Map of Galway in 1610. *Fac Simile of the Original.*

CITIE OF GALWAYE

1610

Speed map of Galway, 1610

they were proud merchant princes; to the de Burgos they were a treacherous mafia; to the Irish they were old English; and to the new Protestant English they were Catholic and adopted Irish. They professed loyalty to the English throne, yet openly traded with and gradually adopted Irish manners and customs. They remained royalist and loyal to Rome, even when Galway officially converted to Protestantism at the end of the 1500s. Despite their conflicts, they were responsible for developing the city and creating its first golden age.

The English

The new English, as they were known, arrived in Galway in the wake of the Cromwellian siege of the city in 1652 and effectively took charge of the governance from the merchant families. In contrast to the original founders of the city, the new settlers were Protestant and adapted a very hardline attitude to the Catholic religion, which led to the closure of many religious houses and the forced removal of many Catholics from that time. Consequently, the centuries of prosperity and local authority ended as the new order took control of the town's commercial, administrative and religious affairs. The city stagnated through the lack of a charter which guaranteed revenue and, following the Williamite wars of 1691 and subsequent Penal laws, went into decline in the seventeenth century.

The new Protestant rulers governed the town despite being a small minority of the population and many were not of wealthy means. They raised tolls and taxes on all trading goods to generate income, which only succeeded in the Catholic majority operating a contraband trade, which deprived the Corporation of much needed revenue. Thus, the Golden Age of Galway's prosperity ended and did not recover until towards the end of the twentieth century. The most prominent of the new English families were the Eyre family, after whom Eyre Square was named. They were staunch, puritan Protestants, but resourceful entrepreneurs and attempted to improve the condition of the town, including developing a new quay and dock for shipping at the Long Walk. During the eighteenth century, religious intolerance towards the Catholics relaxed and their numbers increased again, outnumbering the falling Protestant population of 350 by forty to one. In the nineteenth century, a second wave of English entrepreneur settlers, such as the Persee family, developed mills, distilleries and breweries, which provided the majority of the employment around the time of the Famine. However, with the rapid decline of the town in the latter part of the nineteenth century, due to the Famine, and with the formation of the new state in the early part of the twentieth century, the Protestant ruling class gradually left the city and became dispersed to England and its colonies.

The Religious Orders

The range of religious orders who came to Ireland from Europe in medieval times reciprocated the flow of Irish missionaries who preached and taught in Great Britain and Europe in Early Christian times. The particular orders who settled in Galway reflected the fact that Galway was one of the two Irish ports serving the medieval pilgrim route to Santiago de Compostela in Spain. The orders not only brought spiritual guidance to the citizens of the city, but were also involved in education and caring for the sick. Some of the orders, such as the Carmelites (1641) and the Capuchins (1643), failed to survive the Williamite wars at the end of the seventeenth century, while others such as the Cistercians had only a detached presence in the city, through St. Nicholas' Church, which was a dependant of their monastery in Abbeyknockmoy in north east County Galway until 1484. All the Catholic religious orders had troubled histories in the town because of the sequence of religion wars that originated in England from the fifteenth century. Today their presence in the city is represented by the range of buildings and friary settlements, which continue to give certain parts of the city a particular association and history. Many of them provide Galway with the last remaining, living, insti-

Poor Clare Convent – An oasis in the city centre

tutional connection to its medieval past and interrupted history, and for many citizens of the city make a major contribution to its sense of place.

The Franciscans

The Franciscans, founded in Italy, were brought to Galway by the de Burgo family and established a friary on St. Stephen's Island in 1296 near the Little gate tower of the medieval walled town (now occupied by the Court Houses). Containing about twenty friars, the original friary extended to over three acres, but is now reduced to the Franciscan (Abbey) church in Francis Street. The area around the Abbey became the first Franciscan parish in modern Ireland in 1971. The related Poor Clare or Franciscan convent, originating in France, was established in 1649 in what is now known as Nun's Island. They are an enclosed, contemplative order devoted to prayer and sacrifice, and the early nineteenth century convent on the original grounds is still in use.

The Augustinians

Originating in Italy, the original Augustinian Friary was established at Forthill in 1508, but had a difficult history. In 1589 it was the burial site of the 300 surviving Spanish Armada sailors who were executed by the British forces. Because of its strategic hilltop position between the land and port entrance to the town, it became a walled-in fort in 1602, but the entire monastery was demolished prior to the Cromwellian siege of the city. The Augustinian's eventually settled in Middle Street, in the eighteenth century and are represented today by the Augustine Church, which was rebuilt in 1855.

The Dominicans

Founded in France, and the order most associated with the Claddagh, the Dominicans established a friary at St. Mary's on the Hill overlooking the current Dominican church in 1488, which was granted priory status in 1612. The associated Dominican Nuns established a convent in 1643 and opened a convent school in 1858 on Taylor's Hill, which catered for boarding and day pupils and remains a popular primary and secondary school to this day.

The Jesuits

Founded in France and Italy, the Jesuits came to Galway in 1620 and established a school within the walled town in 1640. Forced to leave during the Cromwellian and Williamite wars, they returned in 1727 and eventually opened a school in Eyre Square. They moved to their present location on Sea Road in 1860, where they later taught through Irish and eventually became a co-educational school in 1974.

The Americans

Galway's relationship with America developed slowly and gradually from late medieval times, unconscious almost at first, but increasingly more direct as history and circumstances cemented the connection. The first interface occurred during the sixteenth and seventeenth centuries as Galway Port traded with a number of American ports. The eighteenth and nineteenth centuries changed the link from goods to people, with the waves of emigration from Galway, particularly in the post-famine era. The sea routes between both countries consolidated their relationship in the first half of the twentieth century with cruise ships to Galway Port conveying the Irish American community re-visiting their ancestral roots and conveying further emigrants on their return. The funding of Galway Cathedral by the Irish diaspora in America symbolised the economic links, while the visit of American Presidents John F. Kennedy and Ronald Reagan to Galway in 1963 and 1984 symbolically embodied the human link. In an ironic reversal in 1971, the Americans arrived in Galway offering employment, instead of Galwegians travelling to America seeking it.

Galway's growth in the last fifty years was underpinned by a strongly performing industrial sector, seeds of which were sown with the development of Galway's first industrial estate in Mervue in 1967. The driver of that growth was the arrival of Digital Equipment Corporation from America, then the world's second largest computer manufacturer, which, attracted by the country's low tax rate, start-up incentives and skilled workforce, established a plant in Mervue in 1971. Their presence in Galway had widespread implications for the city, both visible and hidden. The company would go on to employ 1,200 people directly, 1,300 people indirectly, impacted second-hand on a further 4,000 to 5,000 people, and

The former Digital plant, now Boston Scientific

would become synonymous with the city, becoming embedded in its employment and commercial identity. They developed a computer literate expertise within the workforce, which would provide dividends when the plant closed twenty-two years later. They interacted with both National University of Ireland Galway and Galway–Mayo Institute of Technology in sourcing a skilled workforce and shared common interests. Finally, and most importantly, they raised the profile of Galway as a good place to set up business.

The herd mentality encouraged their peers to follow. Since then, further American companies in the computing, communications, healthcare and other fields have established a cluster of plants in Galway, including Boston Scientific, Medtronic, Tyco, Hewlett Packard, Cisco, Avaya, Fidelity, American Power Corporation, Merit Medical, Bechman Coultar, Thermo King and Bioware. These often silent, background companies are now the single biggest sector contributors to the local economy and maintain its employment profile in high-end skilled jobs, many with a research and development base. Ironically, the closing of the Digital Plant in 1993, which at the time appeared to have the same negative impact as the Ford closure in Cork or the Dell closure in Limerick, had the opposite effect. The skilled workforce set up their own enterprises and the city developed a confidence from overcoming the setback. For Galway, America was an outlet at the end of the nineteenth century, but by the end of the twentieth century and into the twenty-first had become a welcome invitee.

The Tourists

Tourists now come to Galway to enjoy, amongst other things, its sense of place, often unaware that they are now part of the story. Each year, Galway attracts in the region of two million visitors, or in comparative terms, about thirty times its resident population of 75,000. It has a nine month extended tourist season extending from March to November, with a high concentration during the three summer months. Consequently, at various times during the intense holiday period Galway's population is doubled through visitor numbers, which naturally has a big impact on its sense of place.

The story of Galway's tourist industry is linked to the story of transport. Being an isolated west coast city, Galway was dependant on transport modes. The tourist industry started to emerge with the coming of the railway in 1851, which reduced travel time from Dublin from days to hours. With the railway came Galway's first hotel, the Railway Hotel, also built in 1851 and now renamed the Meyrick Hotel. Initially, tourism was driven by the seaside resort of Salthill and the wider attraction of Connemara. Scheduled sailings between Galway and America at the end of the nineteenth century added to the slowly developing industry and the cruise liner business peaked during the 1930s. Overall, tourist numbers to the city were small and it wasn't until the 1960s and the growth in air travel and, in particular, the development of Shannon Airport, that Galway's visitors started to increase significantly. The growth was reflected in the huge increase in the number of hotels, B&Bs and hostels, increased summer traffic and the general realisation that the visitor market to Galway could be cultivated in different ways. Ironically, over 100 years after

Visitors to the city for the Volvo Ocean Race

the birth of the business the trend reversed, with the city centre becoming the focus and the popularity of Salthill waned due to the attraction of cheap foreign sun holidays.

Today, tourism is one of Galway's biggest economic sectors, attracting visitors primarily from Great Britain, Continental Europe and North America. It is now the industry that now most defines the city and which has created its brand image, that of being a tourist magnet. That image is centred on a strong festival calendar from March to November rendering it a veritable festival city. These festivals, including the St. Patrick's Day Festival, Comedy Festival, Cúirt International Festival, Early Music Festival, Galway Sessions Festival, Film Festival, Arts Festival, Macnas Parade, Galway Race Festival, Jazz Festival, Oyster Festival, Baboró Festival and Tulca Visual Arts Festival have succeeded in transforming 'the city of the tribes' into a bustling 'city of the vibes' during the extended tourist season. Tourists are now a major contributor to Galway's physical and social sense of place, impacting directly or indirectly on the range of building types, commercial outlets, businesses and cultural attractions that the city now promotes or provides.

CREATED IN STONE

> 'The town is small but has fair and stately buildings. The fronts of the houses (towards the street) are all of hewed stone up to the top, garnished with fair battlements in a uniform course as if the whole town had been based on one model.' – c. 1614 Description of Galway.

> 'It is built upon a rock, environed almost with the sea and the river, compassed with a strong wall and good defences after the ancient manner.' – St. Oliver St. John, 1640

> 'A grey city set among many abounding waters with an air of stony permanence that refuses to die.' – Robert Lynch, 1912

In contrast to the three other major cities in Ireland, Dublin, Cork and Limerick, Galway's historic, centre part of the city is built exclusively in stone. The seventeenth century description of being 'based upon one model', or the twentieth century description of 'uniquely grey', still holds true. Consequently, Galway's built city has a similarity and uniformity

1820 illustration of St. Nicholas' Church

which derives from its basic construction component, which is stone. Whilst the relatively recent practice of rendering over stonework, dating back to the nineteenth century, has masked this characteristic somewhat, it fails to conceal the extensive use of stone in constructing the city and its impression of 'stony permanence'. Indeed the bumpy nature of some of the render and the occasional exposed feature stone, usually carved, is both a reminder of the underlying core material and a homage to its potential and tradition in the city. The even more recent trend of colourful painting, over the render finish, dating back to the middle of the twentieth century, further confuses the visual impression of Galway's stone heritage and reflects a desire to brighten and contrast the combined background of grey skies and grey streetscape.

The use of stone in constructing the city was not confined to buildings only. Boundary walls, quay walls, canal walls, monuments, paving, roofs and floors all point to the flexible and enduring use of stone in the city, creating a tough, grey and durable backdrop onto which more delicate layers were added, all to accommodate human occupation and activity. Its use in Galway provides a variety beyond building type and age, and in both its casual and formal use gives the city a certain grounding and potency. More than any other material, stone identifies the imprint of successive human endeavour in the city and, following its trace, goes to the roots of its identity.

Galway's distinctiveness in terms of its stone heritage is not confined to the visual, overground built city. The city has also a unique underlying rock geology, which distinguishes it from other cities in Ireland. Galway is built on the geological dividing line between two distinctive underlying bedrocks, the limestone bed to the east of the city and the granite bed

Middle Street

to the west. And because the structure and form of the landscape is based on a single process – the interaction between water and the underlying geology – it is the primary contributor to the divergent landscape of both regions. The brown alkaline earth soil provides the well drained, fertile lands of east Galway, stretching to the River Shannon, and the wet peat, acid soil, provides the barren, mountainous boglands of west Galway, stretching across Connemara to the Atlantic Ocean. It is as if the stone strata has created a story of two cities and two counties in one.

However, within the city itself there is a third distinctive element in its association with stone, which the River Corrib estuary at low tide occasionally reveals to the curious eye. Uniquely in Ireland, Galway is built on, and straddles, the three generic rock groupings found in Ireland – igneous to the west city, sedimentary to the east city and metamorphic the city centre. While sedimentary corresponds to the limestone east and igneous to the granite west, the metamorphic rock consists of the much older and much harder gneiss stone, known locally as green granite, coincidentally and appropriately corresponding to the oldest part of the city and sharing the same family characteristics as green Connemara marble of the higher mountainous regions of that area. So while Galway both connects and divides the county in terms of its geography and geology, the city itself is built on, and also linked and separated by, the trio of Earth's basic bedrocks, with different characteristics, properties and age.

Nature of Stone

Stone is the most basic, widespread and natural material available. Whether near land or sea, stone in varying types, sizes and colours can be found. It is also the most durable, natural material as characterised by the standing ruins of buildings and the uncovered foundations of ancient ones. Its quality of durability has ensured its use for over 5,000 years for all forms of construction from ancient burial graves to cottages, from field boundary walls to elaborate castles, from monuments to public buildings and from tombstones to grand houses. Stone has offered shelter from the climate, protection from enemies, housed gods, reflected the wealth of kings and recorded the coming and going of seasons. It has been used to make tools and weapons of war, to make the wheel to grind corn, to carve and to sculpt and to commemorate the honoured and the dead. Because of its resistance to decay, it continues to provide the primary answer to all the secrets of Galway, back to its foundation in the twelfth century. The recently excavated stone foundation of the Red Earl Hall in 1997 on Druid Lane reveals its history, dating back to approximately 1271, making it the oldest excavated building in the city. Since then all subsequent surviving buildings or ruins can be dated from its stonework, construction and pointing style, including finish, stone features and carvings, representing the various influences expressed by the city during its evolution.

Besides its quality of impervious durability and widespread availability, it had other features that made it imminently suitable for construction. Its small size made it transportable, though generally only locally. It was a very flexible and adaptable material in that it was suitable for

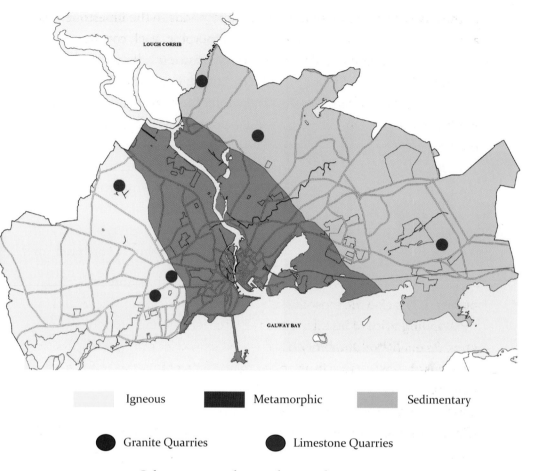

| Igneous | Metamorphic | Sedimentary |

Granite Quarries   Limestone Quarries

Galway stone geology and quarry locations

moulding into different building forms and, more importantly, it allowed the ease of grafting on, for modification or extension to existing structures, like a tissue of skin which in time blends seamlessly in with the existing skin. It was also suitable for renewal or transformation, capable of being used, reused, demolished, stored and recycled at will. Old stone ruins were often taken down carefully, sometimes transported a distance and reassembled to create a new structure and new life, like a skeleton reduced to its individual bone parts and put together, with flesh added, to form a new body, which in time and in the company of human presence also took on a new soul. Finally, as a material it could be carved for decorative or sculptural purposes, or to denote a particular purpose or function.

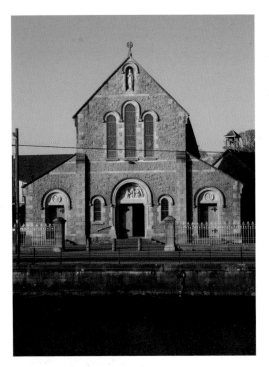

*Dominican Church, The Claddagh,
constructed in granite*

*Lock House, Dominick Street,
constructed in gneiss stone (green granite)*

Stone is deeply embedded in the Irish conscience, a diverse symbol of ancestry, history, spirituality, endurance, but above all both a tangible and subliminal connection to the past and a permanent marker in memory. The decoration, carving and sculpting of stone to elevate it above the mere function of strength, stability and shelter, was a signature in time of an individual or society's pride and expression, sometimes borrowed or adapted, sometimes innate or native, similar but more permanent than the flourish of language, the ornamentation of music and the improvisation of dance.

The attraction of stonework lies in its ageing quality, where the newly quarried or constructed stone soon adapted to its new climatic environment and gradually took on the weathering and patina of age. Similar to the way excavated stone can date a building, exposed stonework can also reveal its age and providence. The beauty of stone is in its expression, where one can follow the trace of the human hand, with each stone individually observed, selected, altered and finally laid in response to the stonemason's eye and fingers. In that way, each stone building is handmade and carries the style and handprint of the mason's craft.

Galway Stone

The use of stone in Galway can be classified into two different groupings: the primary stone for building construction, and carved stone for elements such as doors and windows, or stone sculpture, inserted in various parts of the building fabric.

The primary determinant in Galway's construction in stone was the wide availability of the material locally and the inherited skills of native stonemasons to work with the material. Galway had a series of quality stone quarries, close to and surrounding the city, and the most widely used ones were the limestone quarries at Menlo, Angliham and Merlin Park to the east of the city and the granite quarries at Shantalla, Taylor's Hill and Ballagh to the west. Limestone was the most commonly used stone because of its ease of use and was immensely suitable for cutting, shaping, carving and sculpting. The older granite stone was also used but in far less quantities due to its increased hardness. The oldest gneiss stone found little favour with the builders of the city due to its extreme hardness and difficulty to work with, where even in recent years its removal within the city centre area to create the foundations of new buildings was a major challenge. As well as constructing the city, the local limestone and granite were used in other locations in Ireland, particularly in Dublin, and exported extensively to Great Britain and the continent.

Galway's association with stone is also linked to the craft of local skilled stonemasons. The stonemasons had a particular

1820 illustration of Lynch's Castle

Nun's Island Theatre, constructed in limestone

valued place in Galway life. The craft of stone building involved timeless skills, built up by years of experience and handed on from generation to generation through the close relationship between the master stonemason and the apprentice learner. These skills, whilst traditional, were also adaptable, with the ability to absorb knowledge and accommodate new styles, trends and influences, particularly from successive waves of Anglo Norman and English settlers. Stonemasons had their own guild, dating back to medieval times, a product of the Anglo Norman system of urban administration. Historically, a stone artisan was admitted to the guild on completing his apprenticeship. Stonemasons also had their own language, which also distinguished them from all other craft workers and artisans and made the single biggest contribution to the building of the city. Stonemasons often had their own stonemason's mark, which identified the work of the individual mason, of which there are several examples in Galway city from the sixteenth to the eighteenth century. The stonemason was unique in the community of tradesmen because, above all other skills, their craft was to remain visible, a display of permanent pride for themselves and a source of admiration by successive generations.

To understand the story of the construction of Galway in stone, it is easier to separate it into three different but related parts.

Raw Materials

The primary wall material was the stone itself, of which limestone was the predominant type used. The stone had two different types of origin in the city, those originating in the three major quarries located in the east of the city and stone generally found by simply excavating under the top soil, or as a result of modification to the land over centuries. These origins provided two different categories of stone in the city – rubble stone and cut stone. Rubble stone was stone found in its natural state and although carefully selected for its size, shape, proportions and colour, was not generally altered prior to its use or laying. Cut stone was generally higher quality stone, extracted from recognised stone quarries and was cut and shaped at the quarry as required by the stonemason. The quality of the stone ensured that it generally came in large sizes, free from structural or visual flaws, and behaved in a consistent manner when cut or worked. The use of rubble or cut stone was determined by the hierarchy of building types, from modest dwellings constructed in rubble stone, up to merchants' houses or public buildings constructed in cut stone, with the choice of stone reflecting the status and social standing of the building. From the seventeenth century onwards, cut stone with extremely

Lime kiln at Fishery's Field

fine jointing, known as ashlar, became popular, particularly in the major civic buildings.

The second key ingredient was lime mortar, the adhesive and bonding agent that bound all the stones together when laid. The origin of lime mortar is uncertain, but it is generally acknowledged that its use was brought into Ireland in the ninth century by either the Norse settlers or Irish Christian monks returning from Europe, where it was first used during the period of the Roman Empire. Lime mortar was made up of three ingredients: lime, sand and water. Lime was a white powdery material extracted from a process where broken limestone was burned at a temperature of 900^0 centigrade, using either layers of peat or timber as the burning agent, in a specifically constructed lime kiln, which was normally a pit excavated in the ground, lined and enclosed in stone. The only surviving kilns in the city are in Terryland, just off the Headford Road, and a large, possibly commercial one at the Fishery's Field near NUIG, both of which are protected structures. Besides mortar, lime was also used as a fertilizer and to provide a whitewash, protective coating on walls. The second ingredient in lime mortar was fine sand, taken from the various limestone quarries or specific gravel quarries, where the larger stones were removed from the gravel by sieving to give a small particle sand. The final ingredient was water, always freshwater taken from the River Corrib or Lough Corrib, or gathered from rainfall in large open containers.

Construction

The construction of all walls within the city core followed a similar pattern and construction technique from the thirteenth to the twentieth century. This technique, mainly of native origin but developed by successive Norse and Norman expertise in building and construction, and subsequently adapted by local stonemasons and passed on to later generations, remained virtually unchanged in over 600 years of the city's evolution. Walls were generally constructed 450 to 600 millimetres thick, and occasionally up to 900 millimetres, in a double wall technique, consisting of an outer and inner stone face, normally separate and tied together at intervals with bond or through stones, which penetrated most or all of the

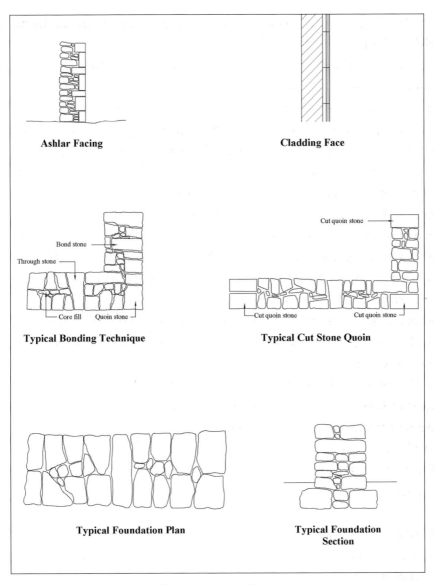

Ashlar Facing

Cladding Face

Bond stone

Through stone

Core fill   Quoin stone

Typical Bonding Technique

Cut quoin stone

Cut quoin stone   Cut quoin stone

Typical Cut Stone Quoin

Typical Foundation Plan

Typical Foundation Section

Stone construction

stone wall and laid in lime mortar of various thicknesses, depending on the quality and shape of the stone. The centre core of the wall was generally filled with smaller stones, also in lime mortar or occasionally mud, to fill the void and to bond both faces of the wall. The resultant wall was structurally very strong and could be built to a height of four to five storeys, sometimes reduced in thickness at intermittent floor levels, as the wall ascended to the top. This basic technique was even used in the construction of the medieval city wall surrounding the original town, as revealed during the development of the Eyre Square Shopping Centre in 1989, when part of the few remaining remnants of the city wall collapsed during construction. All walls were generally widened at the foundation level to spread the load of the wall and commenced on relatively good bearing soil, conditions that were determined by study, knowledge and experience. Despite that, large stone buildings could take up to a generation to settle before forming a stable construction.

Stone Styles

There are approximately ten stone styles evident in the construction of the city since medieval times, depending on the period of construction, purpose of the wall, status of the building and foreign, borrowed or modified influences. These styles are summarised below.

Rendered Random Rubble Stone

This is the most prevalent stone wall classification in the city. The walls were constructed with rubble stone, laid in a random pattern and subsequently rendered with a wet dash consisting of three coats of lime plaster, made up of lime putty, sand and water. The lime mortar provided an extra weathering protection to the building, whilst still allowing the stone walls to 'breathe' and dry out after exceptional rainfall. The more recent trend of removing the render to expose the stonework underneath is not always recommended, as the underlying rubble wall and in particular the lime mortar joints were generally not constructed for that purpose, leading to rain penetration, damp ingress and deterioration of internal plasterwork and paint. Occasionally the render finish was lined to make it resemble an ashlar or a cut stone building. The practice of limewashing with either a natural lime wash (whitewash) or a pigmented wash was primarily a rural cottage tradition and not used to any great extent in Galway City.

Uncoursed Random Rubble Stone

This is the second most common style of stonework in the city, but was still generally rendered on its internal face. The wall was constructed similarly to the rendered wall, but with a more careful selection of the

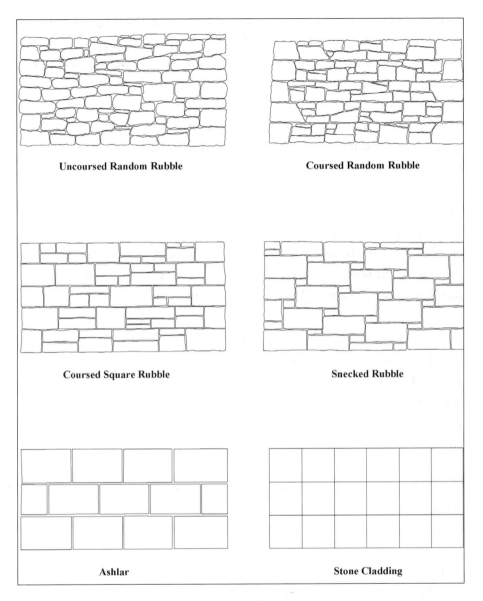

Stone styles

stone for the external face, larger and of better quality, proportion and shape, to reduce the extent and thickness of mortar joints, leading to a more weather resistant stone. Occasionally exposed stones were tilted outwards to throw off rainwater, which all helped to minimise the exposure of the weakest element of the wall, which was the jointing.

Nineteenth century stone streetscape of St Augustine Street

Coursed Random Rubble Stone

Less popular, but still very evident in a large number of locations in the city, this style consisted of the normal, random rubble wall, but built in horizontal courses to a set height averaging 450 millimetres. The technique allowed a break to be formed at the end of a day's work, or where there were a number of different stonemasons working on the same wall, where the horizontal course provided a visual separation between time periods and possibly personal styles adopted by different masons.

Coursed Square Rubble Stone

In this style, each stone was squared to give a more regular appearance and to allow finer jointing to be achieved.

Square Rubble Coursed Stone

This style consisting of similar sized rubble stone that was generally squared all round and laid in a regular pattern. This style of rubble stone is the closest to the cut or ashlar style of stonework.

Snecked Rubble Stone

Similar to coursed square rubble stone, but with smaller stones or snecks introduce to break joints and to use all available stone sizes to eliminate waste.

Random Rubble with Cut Stone

A common wall type in Galway, consisting of a standard random rubble wall with cut stone introduced at weak points such as corners of buildings and edges of windows and doors, both as a structural and decorative feature.

Cut Stone

Also known as ashlar, this is the prime stone style, using quarried stone of high quality, precisely cut and shaped by the stonecutter for laying by the stonemason with extremely fine joints. Regarded as the premium stone construction method, it was also the most expensive due to its high labour requirements and quality of stone used.

Carved gargoyles on St. Nicholas' Church

Decorated Cut Stone

This style covers a wide range of surface finishes, decoration, carving and sculpting, covering various periods and styles from the medieval period to the twentieth century. Decoration varied from simple surface finishes on the stone, using different tooling techniques such as hammering, punching and tooling, to elaborate carvings and sculpting of the stone to create a range of visual effects from the very basic to the highly embellished, including carved door and window surrounds, carved keystones and chimney pieces to sculptured gargoyles. A lot of the stone carvings in Galway consist of heraldic panels and merchant marks – a form of individual signature stamp which helped identify ownership,

Medieval carved stone doorway on High Street

with Galway having one of the largest collections of medieval and late medieval examples in the country, in terms of range and quality. Besides coats of arms, the next biggest category of stone art are those that depict natural foliage, while animal and human scenes with geometric patterns are also prominent.

The body of stone carvings provide an insight into the traits, attitudes, values and personality of the period, and also the depth and extent of continental influences in the city, both direct and transmitted through Britain and adopted or modified locally. One unique and curious feature of decorated stone in the city is the extent that carved stone elements were reused or recycled in successive rebuilding of the city over centuries, either in the same general location or often remote from its original existence, like a nomadic remnant of the city's built past. This feature demonstrates the attachment and importance of sculpted stone and a wish to pay due homage to both its creator, origin and place in the history of the city. Their reuse in a new structure, which at times appears as a mere appendage to the building, acting as both a tombstone to its past life and a birthstone to a new life, often with just a simple desire to raise the building above the ordinary and commonplace.

Stone Cladding
In the second half of the twentieth century there was a marked change in the use of stonework in the city in terms of origin and construction. Increasingly, stone buildings were built with a non-structural stone facing onto a load bearing wall. The facing took the form of a single narrow face of rubble stone, fronting a block wall or a thin cut stone cladding fixed to a concrete or block structural wall with stainless steel brackets and minimal mastic jointing. The origin of the stone also changed with local stone no longer enjoying exclusive usage. Today, modern cut stone cladding is imported from Italy, the Iberian peninsula, Scandinavia, South America, South Africa and increasingly from China.

Maintenance, Light and Colour
Because of its durability, stonework in Galway has required very little maintenance. However, because of the city's exposure to the prevailing southwest winds, the weakest element of the stone construction, which is the pointing, requires replacing or repair over time, particularly on the exposed southwest facades. A lot of the re-pointing is inappropriate, con-

sisting of raised instead of the traditional recessed pointing, which best reveals the character and nature of the stone and is not as prone to damage by the elements. Whilst the colour of the stone-constructed city is grey and often appears to be in sympathy with the leaden skies overhead, under varying sky conditions and at particular times of the day and year, it takes on a range of hues. Galway is noted for the ever changing pattern of its western light like a giant theatre of direct, subtle or diffused shimmerings, which creates a varying and at times mystical townscape, that both delights and inspires. This quality of natural light, in particular under sunshine and cloud conditions in spring and autumn, stone can take on a luminous quality, which seems to contradict the very nature and essence of the material itself.

DEVELOPMENT OF THE CITY

Galway's origin, evolution and growth as a city were determined by its river estuary and coastal setting, its relative isolation on the west coast of Ireland, its rugged infertile environs, its delayed entry into urbanism, its long periods of both prosperity and stagnation or decline, the successive political and religious wars, originating in Britain, and the continued occupation of its hinterland by the Gaelic Irish. Besides being the most western city in Europe, Galway was also situated on the boundary line of foreign influences in the country which separated the Viking/Norman penetration and plantation of the south and east of the country from the relatively untouched and maintained culture of the west and north. However, its coastal trading potential eventually ensured the creation of an urban settlement, albeit later than other Irish coastal cities, where in contrast to the Vikings who travelled seaside, the Normans came landside to form a centre of trade. Over the centuries, successive generations used the location to develop the city's varied and complex history shaped by political, commercial, religious, cultural and social influences.

While Galway is always considered the most Irish of cities, it is firmly placed within the tradition of European towns and cities. This tradition, originating in medieval Europe, delayed and filtered through England and finally translated and adapted to Galway's geography, climate and native culture, is the defining factor in its evolution. Despite being the talisman of progress, the growth and success of its trading relationship with Atlantic Europe also exposed the city to direct European trends and fashions, which belied its remoteness at the edge of Ireland and the continent. Contrary to accepted opinion, Galway was affected by the Renaissance. Lynch's Castle is designed in Irish Gothic with Renaissance influences. Galway was also influenced by French and Italian architecture, but contrary to general opinion hardly at all by Spanish. The modification to the European urban tradition to suit local condition gives Galway its distinctiveness as a city, and in the hands of native builders and artisans it took on a unique local flavour characterised by simplicity, sparseness, informality and at times a bit of fantasy.

While it is perceived, portrayed and feels like a medieval city, its streetscape and patterns are primarily post-medieval, although overlaid on the fabric of its medieval base and with a diverse range of medieval remnants. Its medieval feel and the compact, intimate nature of its streetscape also results from the compact size of the original walled town, which remained intact up to the end of the eighteenth century. So whilst the buildings are long gone, the Norman footprint of the walled city is still relatively intact today, although altered and extended at its edges. Consequently, the city core retains the compactness and intimacy of the medieval city. Ironically, its periods of stagnation and decline had as much influence in creating its sense of place as its periods of prosperity. Its stagnation during the eighteenth century resulted in the great Georgian expansion of cities like Dublin, Cork and Limerick, where new streets and squares were added to the existing fabric, completely bypassing Galway and the city became frozen in time. Its century of decline after the Famine period further restricted and confined its evolution and conferred on it the status of provincial town rather than city, which it still displays to a certain extent – a small town wrapped in city clothes.

The Walled Town (1250–1400)

The Normans were expert builders and prolific founders of towns, developed through their experience in South Wales in the previous century, and Galway followed a similar pattern to that of other Irish coastal cities. Favouring river estuary sites for coastal towns because of their strategic

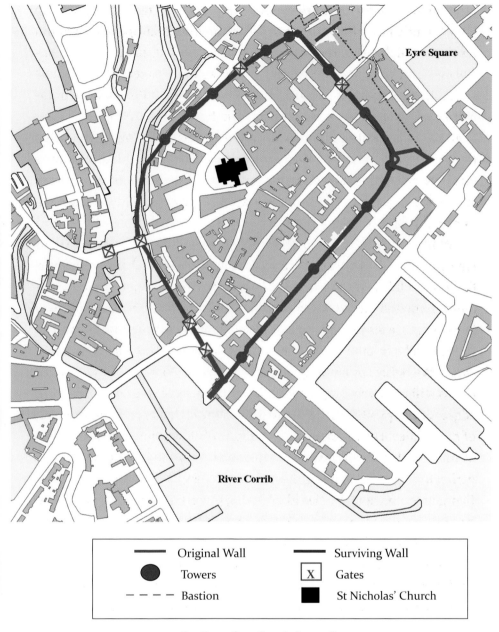

Outline of medieval city wall

trading potential, the Normans laid out the town around the original castle settlement they established in 1235, supplanting the existing Gaelic Irish fort settlement at the ford crossing of the River Corrib. The sole purpose of the town's foundation was profit, through rent, by leasing out the various town plots to the later Norman settlers. The town wall commenced in 1270 and was completed by the early 1400s, funded by taxes and tolls, and enclosed an area of 13 hectares – average for towns, but small by city standards – and its purpose was fiscal and administrative as well as military. The wall eventually had five gate entrances which facilitated the collection of tolls and controlled access to the town – the Great Gate to the east, the West Gate over the River Corrib, the Quay Gate to the port area and two smaller gates to the north and south walls.

Within the walls, the town was laid out in a simple, regular grid pattern which became more irregular towards the West Gate as it forked and curved, possibly due to localised ground conditions. The streets were formed in a linear pattern, generally running east–west with a series of interconnecting lanes and alleyways on a north–south orientation. Besides the existing castle, which was for defensive and administrative purposes, the town was centred on the two focal elements of Norman towns, the market place located at present day Mainguard Street, which allowed for the trading of all goods and services, and St. Nicholas' Church, constructed in 1320, which catered for the spiritual needs of the citizens. The remainder of the town was divided into blocks between streets, which was further sub-divided into plots for individual sites and buildings. The larger houses fronted on to the main street, while the smaller dwellings were found in the lanes and alleyways. Many of the houses were most likely timber frame with thatched roofs, due to the level of forestation and availability of reed locally, however, fires in 1412 and 1473 prompted the use of stone and slate from then on.

The Merchant Era (1400–1650)

The Golden Age of the city extended from the beginning of the fifteenth century to the middle of the seventeenth, and was characterised by growth, prosperity and, in the case of the merchant families, considerable wealth which gradually reflected itself in the city's streets, townscape and buildings. A measure of Galway's rise to prominence during that period lies in the fact that in 1376 the four cities of Ireland were Dublin, Cork, Limerick and Waterford and the five towns were Drogheda, Kilkenny, New Ross, Wexford and Youghal, but by 1650, Galway was second only to Dublin in terms of its economy and strategic importance to the British Crown. During this era, the Norman town grew to a city, built on the pattern as laid out by the Norman's and with all the characteristics of a prosperous urban settlement, large parts of its footprint which remains to this day.

The city enclosed the fourteen streets and fourteen laneways as created by the first settlers, and gradually developed a range of public and religious buildings, including churches, monasteries, friaries, poorhouses and a hospice, plus infrastructural work such as bridges and rebuilding of the town walls. However, it was the continued development of dwellings which was the mainstay of construction activity and which formed the medieval townscape. These generally modest dwellings were punctuated by elaborate townhouses for the merchant families, which occupied strategic positions in the streetscape. The three to four storey fortified urban keep houses were based on the rural Norman castles of the fifteenth and sixteenth centuries, built to accommodate upperclass landlords but with considerable stone carvings and decorations following the trends

and fashion of Europe. A description of the town in 1614 by St. Oliver St. John records its appearance: 'The town is small, but has fair and stately buildings. The fronts of the house (towards the streets) are all hewed stone up to the top, garnished with fair battlements in a uniform course as if the whole town had been built on one model.'

The 1651 pictorial map of the city, which was embellished to give a more flattering representation of the 'perfect city', nevertheless is the most important historical document at a key junction in its history and one of the most fascinating,

Blake's Castle

visual illustrations of an Irish medieval town. The bird's eye view map indicates the town outline and street layout within the city walls, most of which still remain, including St. Nicholas' Church, which dominates the centre of the town, Lynch's Castle, Blake's Castle and the Spanish Arch. It captures Galway at the apex of its prominence and importance at the end of the Merchant Era.

Stagnation Period (1650–1800)

The new Protestant order established after the 1651 and 1691 religious wars led to a reversal in fortunes for the city and a period of inactivity, which paradoxically was the defining era in the city's urban evolution. The era commenced with the destruction of many of the town's buildings in the aftermath of the Cromwellian invasion. With the abrupt reduction in the town's wealth, the era is characterised by the absence of building until well into the nineteenth century. This inactivity explains why Galway has

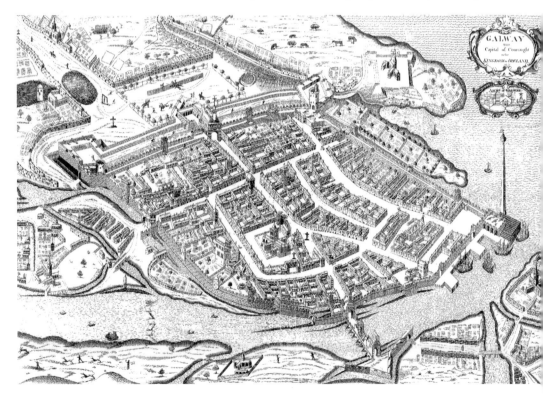

Pictorial map of Galway, 1651

the greatest concentration of sixteenth and seventeenth century houses in the county. Crucially, the stagnation caused by lack of wealth also explains why Galway never experienced the great Georgian period of city building as other cities in Ireland – in particular, Dublin, Limerick and Cork – and why it generally retains its compact medieval layout and network of streets and stone character today. The end of the city's prosperity is captured in D. Beaufont's description of the city in 1787, where he recounts of past stories and 'the house high and very few of them new – but many in absolutely ruin – the entrance into all by a gothic door or stone arch some adorned with pillars and sculpture'.

The only building activity of note during the period was a new Mud Dock at the port, and a Tholsel building for administrative and judicial purposes which was never completed. The only notable buildings of the Georgian period and style built were Mayoralty House and the Bank of Ireland in Eyre Square. Despite the decline, the city's population grew from 6,000 in 1700 to 20,000 in 1800, which led to overcrowded, slum conditions in the old houses of the town. This development prompted the gradual abandonment of the town by the business and merchant classes to the new, more fashionable areas outside the town walls in Dominick Street and Eyre Square. The town walls had fallen into disrepair by 1750 and had all but disappeared by 1800.

Sixteenth and seventeenth century buildings in Kirwan's Lane

Struggle Back to a City (1800-1860)

This period was characterised by a measure of prosperity in the form of industrial and building construction, which led to the town struggling to regain its status and importance as a city and service centre for the hinterland and province. Building activity increased and the city now expanded beyond the town walls following their demolition. A new area known as Newtown Smith with four new streets was laid out in the north of the town, near the Franciscan Abbey, and became the location of the new courthouse. The town also developed westwards towards Dominick Street, and to the east Eyre Square was enclosed. The new prosperity was partially driven by the grain trade, which resulted in numerous mills being constructed adjacent to and powered by the river and its many tributaries, with large warehouses built near Merchants Road and the Docks. Most of the city's public buildings stem from that period. Besides the

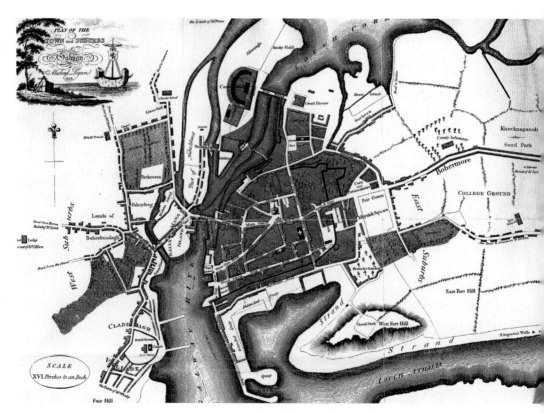

Logan map of Galway, 1818

Typical nineteenth century mill buildings

courthouse, this era saw the construction of the university, infirmary and numerous Catholic churches.

Infrastructural projects were also completed during this time of growth, mainly and ironically around the time of the Great Famine, including the new harbour (1853), the railway (1851) and the canal (1853), plus two new bridges over the River Corrib and the construction of Nimmo's Pier. Many of the existing buildings within the original town walls were rebuilt and some of the streets reformed to a pattern that exists today. New commercial buildings were developed, such as the Meyrick Hotel, Brown Thomas Department Store and bank buildings around Eyre Square. By the time of the Famine, Galway had regained its status as a city and a semblance of its former glory. W.M. Thackeray wrote of the town in 1842:

> *Great warehouses and mills rise up by the stream, or in the midst of unfinished streets here and there, and handsome convents with their gardens, justice houses, barracks and hospitals adorn the large poor, bustling, rough and ready town.*

In 1851 the population stood at 20,500, but the effect of the Famine and the competition brought by the arrival of the railway and new harbour drove the city into an economic recession, from which it took over a century to recover.

Decline and Slow Recovery (1860–1960)

This century in the history of the city is marked by a severe decline from which there was only a very gradual and slow recovery. In the first half of the period, the city declined from a population of 20,000 in 1860 to 13,000 in 1911, and a replicating reversal of its status from a provincial city to a provincial town. The period from the famine up to the foundation of the new free state was again one of building inactivity, with the exception of some infrastructural projects such as the opening of the Galway to Clifton railway line in 1895 and the developing tourism in Salthill. Vast areas of the city, in particular the industrial mills and warehouses, gradually became dormant and the city's footprint and streetscape remained unaltered during this period. There were occasional institutional buildings constructed, such as St. Mary's Diocesan College in 1912, but overall activity was minimal.

The new state's priority in terms of shelter was reflected in the new housing scheme in Bohermore to the east of the city and the Claddagh to the west during the 1930s. Post-World War II, the state's new priority of health was manifested in the construction of Merlin Park Hospital in 1952 and the Regional Hospital in 1956, with additional housing schemes in Shantalla and Mervue. With the oncoming approach of the 1960s and a new outward-looking Ireland, the country's quest for identity and direction, and the tussle between tradition and modernity, were reflected in the design of the Regional Hospital and the new Galway Cathedral commenced in 1957. With the dawn of the modern era, Galway's urban character had been formed by the periods of growth and prosperity (1450 to 1650) and (1800 to 1860) followed by immediate periods of protracted stagnation and decline, which inadvertently helped to preserve the two growth periods as almost museum stage sets in the city's history. The modern era was to usher in the second golden age of the city and bring new changes and new challenges.

GAELIC SETTLEMENTS

Parallel with the evolution of the city on the east bank of the River Corrib, two separate Gaelic Irish settlements were developing in relatively close proximity – the Claddagh village on the west bank of the river and Menlo village on the south shore of Lough Corrib. Very little is known about the origins of both villages, as the only historical documentation covers the 19th century period. However, by the time of the Famine, it is clear that both were substantial settlements with sizable populations and a distinctive village footprint. The villages shared similarities and differences. The basic unit of both was the traditional Irish thatched cottage, all of similar size and design. In the Claddagh, the cottages were linked to form row housing with a similar orientation and a semblance of a street pattern. In Menlo, the cottages remained separate and distinct, with no clear orientation and created an informal, almost haphazard arrangement. While neither village could be described as an urban settlement as such, because there was no hierarchy of building types with a variety of uses such as commercial, educational or religious buildings, nevertheless they indicate a pattern of proximity and density that was approaching an

The Claddagh housing from the 1930s

urban form. Both villages are an interesting study, as they challenge the perception that Ireland had no indigenous, Gaelic settlement tradition (outside of the Viking and Norman urban systems) other than the Early Christian monastic settlements.

The Claddagh

The Claddagh comes from the Irish word *cladach* meaning flat stony shore. Now better known for the Claddagh Ring, which was worn, but not exclusively so, in the area and from where it may not have even originated, its importance lies in its composition, social structure and settlement pattern. The Claddagh was an autonomous Gaelic-speaking community, who devoted their lives to fishing and all activities connected to the sea. They had their own distinctive habits and character in terms of laws and regulation, fishing craft, manners and customs, marriage, amusements and dress. They elected their own mayor and rarely married outside their own community where outsiders were known as 'transplanters'. The origin of the settlement is unknown, although it could have predated the Norman foundation of the city and conceivably as early as the fifth century or even prehistoric times.

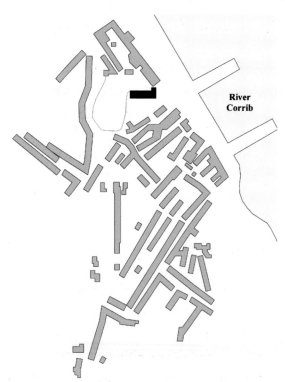

River Corrib

The village was demolished in 1934 and replaced with a new cluster of houses. Whilst photographs and descriptions of the Claddagh prior to its demolition indicate a seemingly haphazard arrangement of traditional thatched cottages, the scale of the community had dwindled considerably by then. Of more interest is the earliest map of the area from 1838 and the very vivid

Layout of Claddagh Village, 1838

description given in Hardiman's *History of Galway* (1820), which indicates a more defined settlement. The drawing as extracted from the 1838 map shows a fairly regular pattern of terraces forming streets and with considerable depth, more akin to an urban settlement. Its more formal footprint than generally assumed was confirmed in Hardiman's contemporary description:

> . . . *irregularly built, but very extensive and intersected with several streets. The number of houses and cabins, which are all thatched, were returned in 1812 at 468 inhabited by 500 families, consisting of 1,050 males and 1,286 females, but the population now, 1820 considerably greater, being supposed to exceed 3,000 souls.*

The described streets and spaces had distinctive names such as Dogfish Lane, Rope Walk Area, Garrai and the Big Grass. What is not known, however, is whether the settlement pattern consisting of streets made up of single storey, thatched terraces was influenced by the adjacent developing city of Galway or did it predate the Normans town. The answer to that question probably lies under the foundation of the existing housing and its secret may be revealed some day.

The Claddagh became well known during the nineteenth century because of the numerous travel writers who wrote about the fishing village and recorded its distinctive and independent way of life. With the growing tourist industry in the twentieth century, the area became immortalised in print, song and story. Today, despite the fact that the traditional fishing village and customs no longer exist, the place name, memory and family connections still do, so it remains a cultural brand for the city.

Menlo Village

In contrast to the Claddagh, where there is a wealth of information from the nineteenth century, there is little historical recording of Menlo village and its inhabitants. Consequently, there is uncertainty about the origin and evolution of the village and the lives of its population. Little is known of the occupation or likelihoods of the citizens, although given its proximity to Lough Corrib it was probably a mixture of farming and fishing. It was generally assumed that the Menlo area consisted of a number of 'clachans', a rundale rural settlement consisting of up to ten inter-

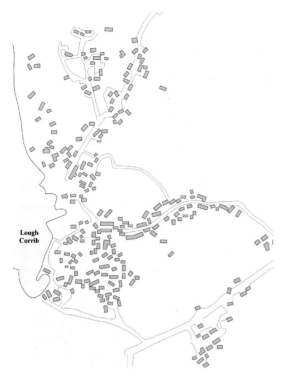

Lough
Corrib

Layout of Menlo Village, 1838

related houses, compactly grouped in an informal manner, which was a feature of rural Ireland, and particularly the west of Ireland, prior to the Famine. However, the 1838 map of the area demonstrates a very different picture. It indicates a very extensive village, comparable to the Claddagh, but much more irregular and sprawling. It appears to show a pattern of settlement that evolved from the clachan system to become a multiple of that basic unit and forming a greatly expanded village footprint. The only vivid picture of the village can be gleaned from the following account of Thomas Foster, London 1846, in his 'Letters on the Conditions of the People of Ireland':

There is no church or chapel in the village, no schoolmaster or doctor or no magistrate, though the population is as large as that of many an English town. The way through the village is the most crooked as well as the most narrow and dirty lane that can be conceived. There is no row of houses or are they approaching a row, but each cottage is stuck independent by itself and always at an acute, obtuse or right angle to the next cottage as the case may be. The irregularity is curious, there are no two cottages in a line or of the same size, dimensions or build. The Irish mind has here without obstruction or instruction fairly developed itself. As it is the largest village I ever saw, so it is the poorest, the worst built, the most strangely irregular and the most completely without head or centre or market or church or school of any village I was ever in. It is an overgrown democracy, no man is better or richer that his neighbour is. It is in fact an Irish Rundale village.

THE MODERN ERA

In Galway's evolution as a city, the fifty-year period from 1962 to 2012 is its most significant phase in terms of its sense of place and our present understanding of it. Galway has changed more in the last fifty years than the previous 500 years in regard to its physical, cultural and economic makeup, which needs to be seen in the national context and the forces that were shaping Ireland as a whole. Ireland in the 1960s was emerging from the sluggishness and inward mentality of the post-independence and post-war years. A new outward looking society began to develop, encouraged by a new political and economic free trade outlook and freedom, culminating in Ireland's entry into the European Economic Community in 1973. The twin engines of social change in Ireland during this period

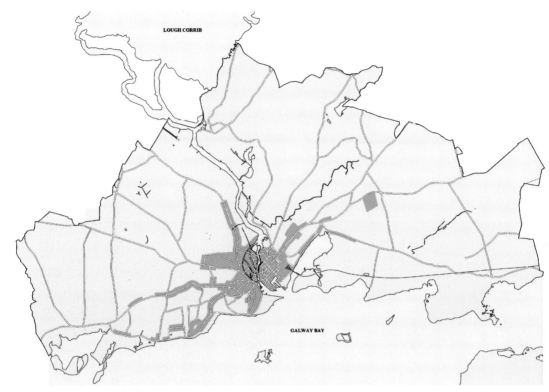

*Map of Galway, 1961/62 – population, 22,000; area, 250 hectares;
density, 90 persons per hectare*

were urbanisation and industrialisation, as the country moved from a
rural-based society, to a city-based one. These changes impacted heavily
on Irish cities, leading to both an expansion and alteration in the nature of
urban areas. The rise in population and employment in cities like Galway
was also accompanied by a culture of car ownership and use, which contributed heavily to the changing character of city life and living.

In terms of planning and change, this period was governed and influenced by two significant piece of legislation, the Planning Acts in 1963
and the Urban Renewal Act of 1986, the former directing and controlling city expansion and the latter encouraging and promoting inner city
regeneration.

Galway city during the fifty-year modern era followed the same pattern and expansion as every other major city in Ireland, influenced by both
Great Britain and America with Dublin acting as the laboratory for the rest
of the country. Consequently, all Irish cities shared broadly similar char-

Map of Galway, 2012 – population, 75,000; area, 2,500 hectares; density, 30 persons per hectare

acteristics, with some local nuances. Galway had the same physical, social and economic growth and change, but it had its own particular experience in terms of tourism and cultural activity. In addition, Galway was operating from a very low base, which is reflected in two startling population figures from census records. From a population of 27,000 in 1821, the number fell to 13,000 in 1911 and did not recover to the 1821 figure until 1971, exactly 150 years later. In contrast, the 2011 census figure of 75,000 is almost six times the 1911 figure, 100 years earlier. In the fifty-year Modern Era, from 1962 to 2012, the population grew from 22,000 to 75,000, an increase of 340 per cent, and consistently boasted of being the fastest growing city in Europe, a dubious honour that nobody questioned or perhaps even checked. The city's growth was characterised by mainly suburban development for the first twenty-five years, which led to a loss in its sense of place, and by ur-ban development for the last twenty-five years, which helped consolidate it again. This duality of city life created in Galway, like elsewhere, a tale of two cities – the visible, public city at the centre and the hidden, private city at the periphery. Galway is now defined and identified by its historic city core, which remains the only focus for visitors to the city. This is not entirely surprising as the centre provides a complexity, diversity and a sense of place that is sorely lacking in its suburban areas.

Suburban Galway

O Rahoon who made you to break the hearts
of young girls with pregnant dreams
of an end terrace, crisp white clotheslines
and hire purchase personalities?
'Ode to the Rahoon Flats', Rita Ann Higgins

While the genesis of suburbanisation and segregation had already been created, by the early 1960s Galway was still a relatively compact city with the working class areas of Bohermore, the Claddagh and Shantalla developed in the aftermath of the new sovereign state, adjacent to the city centre, and the middle classes continuing their drift from the centre, which started in the early nineteenth century, occupying the main entry roads to the city. The process of accommodating the additional city of people numbering over 50,000 involved inhabiting the lands behind and between the approach roads to create new housing areas including Renmore, Mervue, Ballybane, and Terryland to the east and Newcastle, Rahoon, Salthill and Knocknacarra to the west. This resulted in the footprint of the city expanding dramatically on both sides of the River Corrib, consisting of mainly low density housing which was in sharp contrast to the higher density city and inner city suburbs. The stark impact of this type of expansion was the city physically growing three times the rate of its population growth, resulting in the city today having a density of just thirty persons per hectare as against ninety persons per hectare fifty years ago. Thus, during that period Galway moved away from near the European city density norm of a hundred per hectare and closer to the American city density norm of twenty-five per hectare, and became a dispersed, decentralised and deurbanised city.

Almost all of Galway's new housing was to accommodate migration in from the surrounding areas, rather than relocation of the existing

Suburban city

population, in response to new employment opportunities in the industrial, commercial, tourism and state sectors that the city offered. This trend and type of development was encouraged and facilitated by the initial Development Plan for the city which implemented building density standards of six to eight houses per acre, new housing grants and tax relief on mortgages, as against stamp duty tax on existing houses, new improved access roads to and within the city and the Irish love affair with both home and car ownership, which was accompanied by greater affluence, individualism and materialism. The resultant featureless housing estates of bland uniformity caused by repetitive house designs and strict application of road design standards with little sense of place led to difficulties in establishing a sense of community and increased alienation. The semi-detached houses became the ubiquitous house type in Galway and the suburbs.

In hindsight, the subsequent suburban sprawl wasted valuable land, was incapable of being serviced by public transport forcing an increased reliance on the motor car, and was insufficiently dense to support commercial or social services. Uniformity was not just confined to within each estate, but to the collective suburbs and extending to other cities as national house builders provided the same standardised design country-wide, further leading to a lack of regional and local identity. Thus suburban Galway became an 'anywhere, everywhere' settlement area – you could be anywhere because it was everywhere in the country. Galway's suburbs could be described in a similar vein as that of the village settlement of Menlo in 1845, as an 'overgrown democracy' with the key difference being that Menlo was confined and born out of strife and poverty, whilst modern suburbia is extensive and born out of peace and prosperity. This loss of place is typified in Renmore, an area that was the first location for suburban development in the 1960s, which in the fine publication of 2000 entitled *Renmore and Its Environs* sought to establish some sort of identity through their historical heritage and artefacts, now totally subsumed by standard uniform housing.

The negative effects of suburban living was further compounded by the segregated zoning of the city where living and working was separated, again fuelling increased dependency on the car and removing the diversity and complexity of varying uses that makes the city centre so appealing. This is characterised in Galway by all of the segregated industrial and office uses located on the east side of the city, yet more than half of the population residing in the west, leading to extensive cross town, rush hour traffic. The segregation also extended into housing, with separate working class areas established in Rahoon and Ballybane where low car ownership and little public transport resulted in social isolation. This isolation was amplified in Rahoon with the construction of Ballymun-style medium rise apartment blocks, which, besides their unsuitability for their stated purpose, became a highly visual monument to separateness. The fact that they were replaced with standard, low density, segregated housing in the 1990s, whilst understandable, simply repeated the initial poor decision making.

The more recent development plans for the city have recognised and attempted to address this issue by encouraging more placemaking in their approach to creating new housing communities. It is also acknowledged that changing demographics in Galway, where family sizes and units, co-habitation, marriage rates and accommodating the elderly have

Galway 1961/62 – City centre with separate village of Salthill

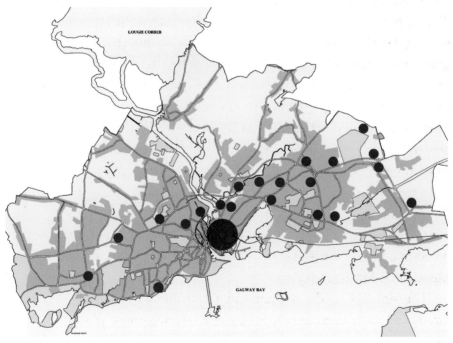

Galway 2011/12 – Multiple centres of activity

led to varying residential unit types and sizes, and where the standard family-sized, three bedroom house is no longer uniformly appropriate. However, these changes are now against a background of a gradual shift in Galway's attitude to housing over the last fifty years where the house has evolved from shelter to home to commodity. Housing has increasingly become part of the 'property market' and seen as an 'investment' or 'asset'. The roots of this attitude lies in two significant changes during the modern era. Firstly, the percentage of public social housing gradually fell over the fifty-year period. Secondly, the quantity of private housing soared, particularly in the last fifteen years, of which only 60 per cent was due to market need, the remainder being market demand for second houses or investment properties. These two changes resulted in seeing housing as a piece of merchandise rather than a social need. Galway has a large transitory population, due to high student and tourist numbers, which combined with the investment mentality has created a burgeoning rental market with increased difficulty in establishing permanent communities with a strong sense of local identity. It is conceivable that the current economic difficulties, combined with property tax and water charges, will impact on Galway's suburban sense of place in the future as it may move towards the more European norm of the home for exclusive personal rather than investment use.

Suburban Shopping and Other Centres

Nothing highlights the change in Galway's sense of place in the last fifty years as the growth in its suburban shopping and other centres. These other centres are a diverse segregated range of mainly economic, but some institutional, centres which are dispersed across the suburban areas and which generate considerable levels of car-dependant activity. These centres include industrial areas, business parks, office parks, retail parks, commercial centres, leisure centres, entertainment centres and greatly expanded institutional centres, all of which were previously located in the city centre and which now create mini-centres throughout the peripheral edge of the city. However, it is the suburban shopping centre that still creates the most public activity. Traditionally, the city core was the sole preserve of shopping options and where all routes led to the

Galway Shopping Centre

centre, becoming the focus and meeting point for both local and rural shoppers. The suburban shopping centre changed that, but also changed the nature and character of shopping. This model of suburban mall was borrowed directly from America, a culture with little or no tradition in European-style urban centres, and translated to the Galway experience.

Galway Shopping Centre on Headford Road, developed in the 1970s, has the distinction of being the first of the species, followed by others at the Westside and Knocknacarra and a later hybrid, the retail park, on the Tuam Road and Headford Road. This type of shopping is dominated by two themes – the car and convenience. In a now car-dominated culture, Galway Shopping Centre became the new shrine, where all shopping could be conducted in one area with car access and car parking given absolute priority. These shopping centres were both facilitated and encouraged by the new cross town, four lane, major arterial roads, without which they could not exist, as that type of model was dependant on being located on major traffic routes, preferably at the intersection of such routes. This new form of modern shopping experience is best illustrated in Galway by the well known Headford Road roundabout, an intersection of two heavily trafficked suburban roads, dominated by the new suburban retailing around it, which are set back from the road to accommo-

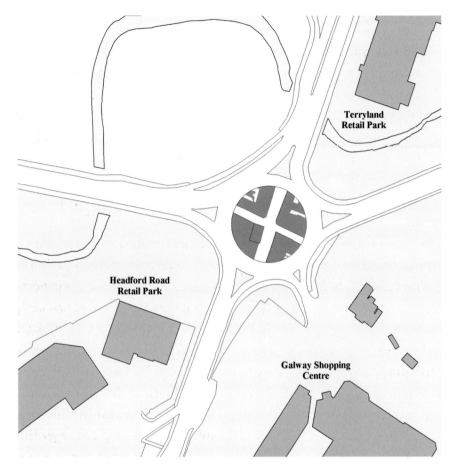

Medieval crossroads of city illustrated on modern crossroads at Headford Road roundabout

date vast areas of tarmacadam car parking. It is both useful and telling to compare this type of junction of roads and retailing with that of the city centre, in particular the junction of Shop Street and Abbeygate Street. In essence, we are comparing the medieval crossroads with the modern crossroads. The same scale comparative drawings of both highlight the difference. The medieval is small, intimate and enclosed with a human scale; the modern is large, disconnected and open with a vehicular scale. In terms of a shopping experience, the modern has swapped conviviality for convenience, joy for joylessness and the human being for the car. In many ways, it is difficult to comprehend that the modern shopping crossroads, compared to the medieval shopping crossroads in Galway, represent 800 years of advances in civilization.

Urban Galway

Similar to the suburban experience, the changes in Galway's city centre must be seen in the context of both national and international trends, and whilst suburban Galway followed a similar pattern to other Irish and even European trends, the urban centre deviated somewhat initially, at least, from the prevailing experience in other cities. Galway and indeed most Irish cities did not experience the post-Second World War rebuilding that occurred in British and European cities. In the modern era, Galway's city core had little of the city redevelopments that took place in other Irish cities, particularly Dublin in the 1960s and 1970s.

By the mid-1980s, Galway in the main had retained its late medieval footprint, which was overlaid with the early nineteenth century period of building activity. This retention was due to successive periods of economic stagnation, and when growth did arrive in the 1960s it was primarily concentrated outside the historic core. Consequently, and now difficult to believe, in 1986 the city centre was being described as a spine of activity and prosperity on Shop Street, behind which lay vast areas of decay and dereliction, mainly industrial-type buildings, underused since the latter part of the nineteenth century. This was the context in which the 1986 Urban Renewal Act was brought into force, to help the regeneration of Irish city centres through tax incentives and relief to encourage redevelopment works. There is still a question mark over whether the motive for the Act was to stimulate building activity or was a genuine interest in revitalising cities. Whichever is the truth, the Act led to the largest reconstruction of the city since the nineteenth century and before that the fifteenth century. The accompanying map shows the extent of development that took place in the city centre in the twenty-five-year period between 1986 and 2011, most of which was concentrated in the years between 1990 and 2000. The largest single development was the Eyre Square Shopping Centre constructed in 1990, which consisted of forty shops, totalling 60,000 square feet of retail space, 30,000 square feet of offices, forty residential units and Galway's first multi-storey car park to accommodate 470 cars, and was seen as a city centre response to the competing growth of suburban shopping centres.

The urban renewal brought many advantages and benefits to the city centre. It shone a light on the city core and gradually opened eyes to the possibility of urban life. It reinforced the centre as the dominant focus of the city after years of suburban weakening of its historical function and role. This was primarily achieved by the provision of new residential units in the city, which reversed the decline of the city centre population, creating a new energetic urban culture and an increase in service and social activities. The redevelopment removed the decades of decay and dereliction, and greatly improved both the image and confidence of the city. It introduced a new generation to the idea of apartment living, a concept generally and previously unknown and unthinkable in the city, and helped to reduce pressure on continued suburban sprawl, thus reversing the relatively recent historical trend.

Urban renewal also had its faults and problems. Redevelopment was confined to residential dwellings, offices and retail use only, with no provision for cultural, institutional or social services use, other vital ingredients in the makeup of a city. In a city with little or no experience of apartments, other than the troubled Rahoon flats, the tax incentives carried no guidelines or minimum requirements for tax-relieved apartments, in particular in relation to aspect or minimum floor, storage and private amenity areas. Consequently, many of the apartments built were substandard and may not have long-term viability. Ironically, many of the later apartments ended up smaller and with an inferior layout to those of the Rahoon flats demolished in the late 1990s. The apartments in general catered for a narrow age and social class, in particular young, single workers or students, which discouraged a broader and more typical city mix. The apartments also cultivated the idea that apartment living was for temporary use as rentals, rather than the possibility of being for a permanent owner occupier. Many were built as gated communities, where security and a fortress mentality developed, which is contrary to the idea and spirit of city living. Tax incentives on all the urban renewal projects impacted on the property market, as the tax relief transferred into higher prices and subsequent land costs, and later formed the benchmark for future land and property costs, even when the incentives were no longer available.

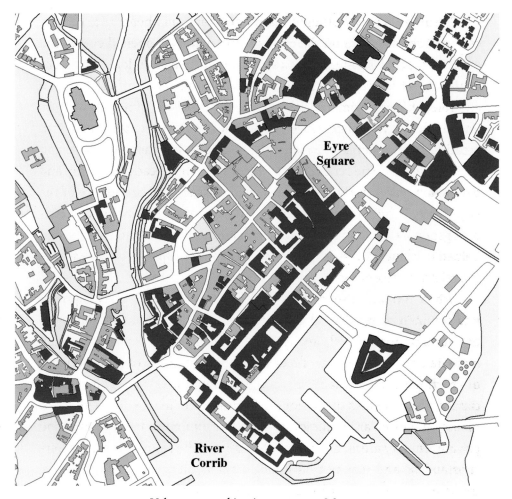

Urban renewal in city centre, 1986–2012

However, the biggest problem with Galway's urban renewal was both the speed and lack of direction or guidance in its implementation. The tax incentive came with a deadline, which gave it a forced haste and lack of consideration, particularly at the larger urban scale. Galway was not prepared, and was not given the resources nor space, to prepare a framework plan for the overall redevelopment of half the city centre. Instead, urban renewal proceeded on the basis of the City Development Plan, which was totally inadequate for such a major regeneration. Consequently, there were huge lost opportunities in creating not just a rebuilt city, but an improved, redesigned city with the emphasis on the quality and linking of urban streets, spaces and amenities. The model for this type of

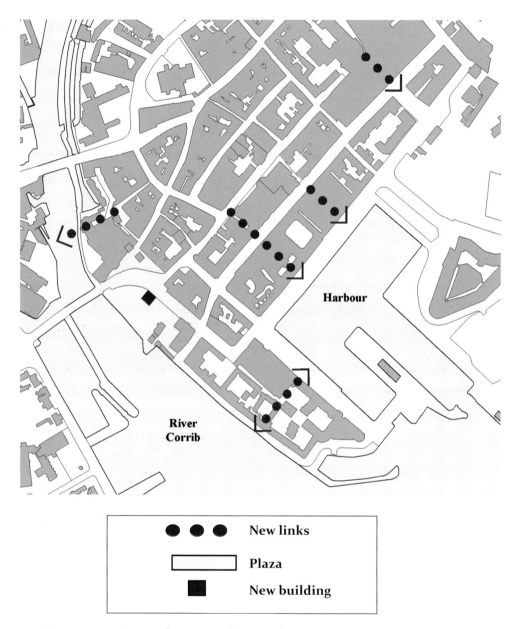

Urban renewal – missed opportunities

approach to the city was the Temple Bar area redevelopment in Dublin, where from 1991, proceeded on the strength of a Framework Plan based on providing new links and streets in that historic area and the provision of a mix of uses, but particularly cultural uses, as the basis for reinforcing its sense of place. Limerick had a similar, but less developed, approach in providing a Heritage Precinct in its historic centre.

Galway required such a framework because of its historical evolution. As noted earlier, Galway as laid out by the Normans within the city walls consisted in the main of a series of parallel streets extending east–west with lanes and alleyways linking them, extending north–south. With the removal of the city wall, the city expanded towards the Docks in the form of further parallel streets, but no interconnecting lanes or alleys because of the nature of the expansion, which consisted of large-scale mills and warehouses instead of houses and shops. The redevelopment of this area during the urban renewal period provided the opportunity to address the lack of connection, which would have had the effect of linking the main pedestrianised spine of the city to the harbour.

In summary, it simply required what the Normans did all of 800 years ago, which was to create an interconnected town. It is an indictment of our progress as a civilized society that in rebuilding half the city centre, equivalent to the size of the Norman walled town, just two new roads for traffic purposes and no new streets were created for pedestrian or civic purposes.

There were other lost opportunities. The Eyre Square Shopping Centre development, the biggest single project, crucially failed to make a link to Merchant's Road and on to the harbour area. Similarly, in Kirwan's Lane the misplaced requirement for a multi-storey car park at the Jury's Hotel site was too insensitive a structure in a historic area and created an impermeable barrier to linking Kirwan's Lane to the River Corrib, resulting in the vehicular entrance for the car park being located beside the remnants of Blake's Castle, the oldest medieval house in the city.

The Fishmarket had the potential to become a far more extensive, appealing and interesting riverside plaza. The lost opportunity here was not in the design of the controversial Portmore development, but the fact that any building was constructed on what was a Corporation owned site. A standalone building with at least a public use on its ground floor would have provided a much more impressive civic public space, more responsive to the adjoining Spanish Arch and Old City Wall, with improved visibility to those city landmarks.

Urban renewal on Merchants Road using historic replication

During the modern era, two significant relocations took place. The Civic Office was moved from the Fishmarket and other dispersed city centre locations and combined in a new building on College Road, which is effectively a suburb of the city. This relocation failed to recognise the importance of sitting such an important public building containing the Mayoral and administrative functions of the city in a more city centre location, as a positive endorsement of the city and a symbolic civic message to its historic core, similar to what both Dublin and Limerick achieved in their relocated civic offices, both on city centre, riverside sites during the same time period. It has resulted in the unusual situation where the County Council offices are closer to the city centre than the City Council offices. The more recent relocation of the new Tourist Office to Forster Street, whilst close to both the new bus station and existing railway station, is a similar lost opportunity in acknowledging the medieval and waterfront city.

Finally, there was a lost opportunity to create a new contemporary architecture in the rebuilding of the city, which was representative of the late twentieth century period, true to its time, whilst acknowledging and reflecting the existing sense of place. A lot of the earlier urban renewal projects looked at the existing historic city as a template for replication, which resulted in a staid, fearful and dishonest architecture and contrary to the spirit and endeavour of previous inhabitants of the city, who left a legacy that reflected their over particular imprint. Some of the later projects sought to introduce a more enlightened, honest approach, but overall the urban renewal experience was a lost opportunity, caused by undue haste, lack of direction and absence of nerve. Despite that, it did help to cement and consolidate the city centre's sense of place. This is not a case of being wise in hindsight. All of these issues were evident at the time but were not exploited due to a lack of a carefully considered framework plan. It is a salutary lesson as Galway expands and develops into the future.

GALWAY'S SENSE OF PLACE

T he historic, city centre's physical sense of place, as created by its evolution from the thirteenth century to the modern era, is characterised by a network of narrow, informal, organic and at times quirky streets and spaces, with a collage of small and tall buildings that range from the medieval to the modern. The buildings vary in period, style and use to give a mosaic that at times is distinct, but also blurred. Some buildings are original replacements of existing ones, but adapted to new uses; others have been extended or modified versions of the original, while some others have been extended and modified numerous

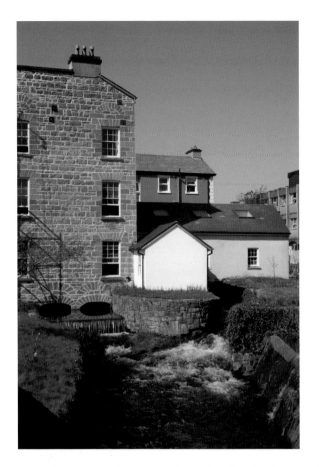

times, each era grafting on to the previous era. The result is layers of history and evolution of different textures, creating a varied townscape of vernacular buildings overlaid onto its medieval legacy. Consequently, there is little uniformity either horizontally or vertically. The streetscape weaves in and out, rooflines jump up and down according to the period, status and use. This pattern is accompanied by an honesty in the architecture, where the buildings, whether house, shop, mill, church or bank, make their own distinctive imprint on the city and coexist, but clearly display their own distinctive use, form and hierarchy.

The streets and open spaces are interconnected creating a varied public sequence of anticipation and surprise for the explorer. Materials also vary, predominantly now facades of render, but with the original stone announcing itself at irregular intervals, mainly in important status buildings, but occasionally in uncovered everyday buildings. Colour is now also a feature, although primarily a twentieth century development. The nineteenth century fashion for plastering was followed by the twentieth century trend for colour, initially restrained by availability, but now released in a riot of tones to enliven the grey render and contrast with Gogarty's 'leaden grey skies'. Surprisingly for a prominent market town, Galway has few decorative, traditional shop fronts, typical of Irish market towns and cities, but instead contains a variety of fronts from the simple to the rudimentary, from the nineteenth century to the modern, which are all part of its own particular distinctive flavour. Indeed, a lot of the buildings could also be described as simple and rudimentary with little of the architectural merit and features of the era, and where even its architectural set pieces such as Eyre Square are somewhat incomplete and incoherent.

However, Galway's sense of place is formed by the collective where the whole is greater than its parts. There are no great statements or gestures, just mainly ordinary, everyday, modest buildings with the occasional flourish or fantasy. In contrast to Dublin or Limerick's great Georgian architecture, it has a townscape that is likeable, rather than necessarily admirable. In essence, its sense of place is shaped by its human scale, which creates the place for human occupation, activity and encounters. The human inhabitation has ensured diversity in the city – a place to live, learn, work, worship, play, entertain and be entertained. It also had a diversity of age, social class and purpose. Outside the historic centre, no Irish city has such an abrupt contrast between its built, dense, enclosed, urban, city core and the natural, wide open vista of the river estuary, inner bay and distant Clare Hills. It remains the only city in Ireland which

suddenly opens itself out to water and the sea, and where the salty Atlantic breezes can be felt and tasted in its medieval streets.

GALWAY'S ARCHITECTURE AND BUILDINGS

Within the general townscape of commonplace buildings, mainly of a simple character, there are occasional flourishes and individual buildings that contribute to the city's sense of itself and its wider external image. These buildings encompass a diverse range of periods, styles, use and cultural associations. The following examples are a representative guide to that diverse stock and are chosen not always on qualitative grounds, but on their particular historical or cultural value to the city and cover mainly public or semi-public buildings from the medieval to the modern.

Because of the city's colonial history, most of the buildings have strong European influences, filtered through England and moulded to Galway's local context. Even after the formation of the state, the city's buildings continued to be shaped by European and increasingly American influences, but now more directly transmitted through Dublin. The more recent examples see the introduction of more regional and national influences, fused with the international. Many of the buildings are for educational or religious purposes, but they also cover the health, commercial, residential, transport, tourist, cultural, justice and defence categories. Critically, all the buildings selected contribute to Galway's sense of place.

St. Nicholas' Church (c. 1350)

The single most important building in the city, because it embodies the very evolution of the city from its birth, through all its fortunes and reversals and, in particular, the political and religious wars that originated in England. Its importance and prominence in both medieval times and today stems from the fact that it is the only building that occupies a full centrally located block in the city centre, which can be viewed in the round and provides a breakout oasis within the dense city core. It is the largest medieval parish church in Ireland and the only medieval ecclesiastical building to survive in Galway. Its large scale results from

St Nicholas' Church

its exceptionally wide aisles, which is reflected in its western triple gable facade, which is unique in Ireland. Dating from the fourteenth century, the church has been subject to numerous alterations and restorations during its 700-year history. Originally a Catholic church and part of the Cistercian Order, it was changed to the Reformed church in 1551, was a Catholic church between 1643 and 1652 and again between 1689-1691, was subsequently a Protestant church and is now a Church of Ireland parish church. The church contains many fine medieval features and monuments, including the south transept window, thirty carved gargoyles to the south aisle, an altar tomb and sixteenth century font. Internally the church has a bright, high airy feel to it, belying its medieval origins, but probably painted at some stage after being transferred to Anglican use in the late seventeenth century.

Lynch's Castle (c. 1500)

Located at the central crossroads of the medieval city, this well-known and much altered town house is characterised by elaborate door and win-

Lynch's Castle

dow surrounds, sculptural stone carvings of various coats of arms and a highly decorated chimney piece in the foyer, which offers an insight into the wealth and prestige of the merchant families during the medieval period. The building's embellishments show a strong continental European influence, in contrast to the sparse simplicity of more typical Irish urban keep house of that time. Used as a bank for almost a century, the building is an important cultural landmark at the four corners of medieval Galway.

Spanish Arch (1584)

More of a structure than a building, the Spanish Arch, which was previously known as the Blind Arch, was built as a fortress bastion to protect shipping and formed an extension to the city wall, part of which survives to the rear. Consisting of a double arch with one arch blocked up, its current name derives from a nostalgic reference to Galway's past trading history with Spain from the old port, which was originally located beside the struc-

Spanish Arch

ture. Today, the Spanish Arch, besides being a focus for tourist activity, provides a strong threshold between the open amenity of the Fishmarket area and the enclosed courtyard of the new City Museum, which further leads to the Long Walk area.

Mayoralty House (c. 1725)

One of the rare and most important buildings from the Georgian period in Galway, it is built in ashlar limestone and displays the typical design feature of that period, including a raised ground floor, projecting central bay, heavy cornice and a simple elegant doorway. The basement level has stone window mullions more typical of the earlier medieval period. Little is known of its architect or its original use, but it forms one of the few focal, axial buildings in the city, terminating the vista at the end of Cross Street.

Mayoralty House

Courthouse (c. 1812)

Designed by Richard Morrison, one of the best known architects of the era, the large imposing courthouse was built on the side of the old Franciscan Abbey. The central doric portico has a uniquely large entablature, which gives the building a weighty and important feeling. The various stone carvings on the cornice and flanking bays include the lion mask and, appropriately, the scale of justice. The building creates an intimate set piece opposite the Town Hall theatre and forms a strong axial relationship with Galway Cathedral to its rear.

The Courthouse

National University of Ireland Galway (NUIG) (1845)

Designed by J.B. Keane, a former assistant of Richard Morrison, NUIG's original quadrangle is loosely based on the Gothic architecture of Christchurch, Oxford in England, consisting of a two storey building around an open quadrangle in the centre. Despite containing many of the characteristics of that style, including turrets, pinnacles and crenulations, some features of the original design were omitted during the construction phase, possibly because of lack of finance. One of the 'Godless' Queen Colleges, as named by the Catholic hierarchy because of its objective to be undenominational, the 'Quad' soon developed an enclave of learning close to the city centre. Today the building is used mainly for administration purposes, as the university has extended northwards, flanking the west bank of the River Corrib.

National University of Ireland Galway

Franciscan Church (1849)

Also known as the Abbey Church, and the finest example of the numerous churches constructed during the nineteenth century, it was designed by J. Cusack and forms part of the streetscape of Francis Street. Entered under a handsome doric portico, the classical style of the exterior is carried into the interior including a doric colonnade, corinthian pediment, ionic side altars and a central coffered dome. The internal layout is similar to the Pro-Cathedral in Dublin.

Franciscan Church

Meyrick Hotel and Railway Station (1851)

Both designed by J.S. Mulvany in the classical style of public buildings of that era, they nevertheless provide an adjacent duality of contrasting scale and context. The five-story Railway Hotel is an imposing building of thirteen bays, dominating the south side of Eyre Square, and was built to a large scale because of the expected tourist business to Galway with the coming of the railway and the construction of the new port. Built in ashlar limestone, heavily rusticated on the ground level, the top floor attic story was added in the 1960s. At the rear side of the hotel is the sin-

Meyrick Hotel and Railway Station

gle story station building with alternating projecting bays, under a heavy cornice and a recessed entrance with a stone canopy above. The iron roof of the station was designed by Richard Turner, the well-known engineer also responsible for the famous Botanic Garden glasshouse in Dublin.

St. Mary's College (1912)

A diocesan secondary school and former seminary college designed by William Scott, it was regarded as a significant pioneering building when constructed. The architectural historian Sean Rothery has referred to 'Scott's highly original design', and noted that 'this building might claim to be the first modern building in Ireland'. Whilst designed in the stripped classical style, Scott's use of cubic forms, flat concrete roof and facade treatment of visually separating structure from infill gives a foretaste of the international style of architecture which was to emerge in Galway over forty years later. The top floor, designed by R. Byrne, was added in 1939, and the south west wing extension was built in 1956 to a design by J.J. Robinson.

St Mary's College

UCHG Nurses Home and Hospital (1938 and 1956)

These two adjoining pioneering buildings, designed by T J Cullen, chart the evolution of the modern international style of architecture in Galway. The Nurses Home is the premier example of the Art Deco period in Galway with the distinctive curved ends, corner windows and a com-

UCGH Nurses Home (top) and Hospital

bination of vertical and horizontal glazing elements. The main hospital building represents the full modern movement expression influenced by European hospital design, and in particular that of the Finnish architect Alva Aalto. With its cubist massing, projecting balconies and horizontal glazing, it represented an interesting example of a new style of public architecture to be adopted by a state struggling with modernist values in a traditional conservative society, yet wishing to sever the link with its colonial past.

Galway Cathedral (1965)

If the new hospital represents the modern outlook, Galway Cathedral represents traditional, conservative values. Designed by J.J. Robinson, it has a traditional cruciform plan based on the liturgical requirements of the 1950s. However, it is the hybrid architecture that attracts the most curiosity, containing an eclectic mix of medieval gothic, European re-naissance – in particular Iberian influences – and small traces of hiberno romanesque. Despite that, it is the immense medieval stoniness of the building, both externally and internally, that is the dominant theme, with

Galway Cathedral

NUIG Arts Block

even the statues of the cross carved in stone, and it remains the last major public building in Ireland to be constructed in load-bearing, structural stonework. The building is characterised by an extremely high quality of craftsmanship and the interior contains a diverse range of late twentieth century artwork by the leading artists of the era. Today, the cathedral is one of Galway's most visited buildings, occupying a prominent focal position on its three approaching axes.

NUIG Arts Block (1972)

Designed by Scott, Tallon, Walker, this is an important essay in the now fully developed international modern style, and in particular the Chicago Miesean School, translated and adapted to the expanding NUIG campus site. The building is characterised by a low level, horizontal podium building, punctuated with vertical tower elements and hollowed out courts, to light up the deep plan footprint. The design is based on a formal, regular planning grid, using a prefabricated modular system which is flexible to accommodate a range of spaces and uses, including student concourse, lecture theatre, teaching areas, restaurant, administration offices and open courtyards. The structural grid is expressed visually on the exterior to create a contemporary classical appearance.

Galway Education Centre (2000)

Designed by de Blacam and Meagher following a Department of Education competition, the building is located on the entrance grounds of a former Redemptorist institutional building, an imposing nineteenth century structure now part of the Galway–Mayo Institute of Technology's School of Art. This intimate building creates its own micro context, using a semi-circular footprint around a circular grassed court, containing a single walnut tree, contrasting with the scale and formality of the existing building. Internally, the accommodation consists of a lecture theatre, library, meeting rooms, IT facilities, cafe and a first floor research gallery. The curved form and simple treatment of building elements creates a modern, monastic centre of learning and an interesting contrast with the original function of the existing building.

Galway Education Centre

Galway–Mayo Institute of Technology

Galway-Mayo Institute of Technology (GMIT) (2003)

Located in a prominent position on one of the major entry routes into the city, GMIT, designed by Murray O'Laoire, provides a new frontage building and image, screening an undistinguished third level college structure dating back to the 1970s. The new accommodation consists of an auditorium, lecture theatre, library and administrative offices. The building's eye-catching feature is the organic, sculptural library corner facade with three dramatic patinated copper sails, reflecting the site's Atlantic exposure and evoking Galway's traditional maritime association – similar to the Eyre Square fountain – which contrasts with the simple, mannered and layered remaining portion of the building. In its short life the building has already established genuine landmark status in the city.

Galway City Museum (2006)

Located opposite the remnant of the city wall and adjacent to the Spanish Arch, the museum, designed by the Office of Public Works, addresses the challenge of placing a contemporary building in a historical setting and the continually evolving nature and purpose of museums. The L-shaped building creates a courtyard entrance plaza fronting and engaging the city wall. Internally, a triple height atrium visually links the three main exhibition levels of the building and highlights the current challenge in modern museum design – the conflict between fixed and flexible spaces and the requirement for multi-functional use. The building utilises the three primary materials of the built city – stone, render and glass – in a fresh way, with a large emphasis on the detailing and quality of workmanship. The views created, in particular of the Fishmarket area and river, suggest that the external city as well as the internal exhibition is also on display.

Galway City Museum

GALWAY'S NEIGHBOURHOODS

While the pedestrian zone in the city centre is the primary symbol of Galway's sense of place, there are numerous other places in the city that contribute to the overall collage, particularly for city residents. These places are diverse and varied in character, containing particular activities and uses or with different physical, built or natural characteristics which help differentiate them from other areas of the city in the mind of locals. Those places form part of the memory of the city, strongly embedded in the conscience of its inhabitants.

Eyre Square

The point of arrival into the city, Eyre Square is both the heart and meeting area of its urban townscape. Public and private buses and trains arrive and depart from beside the square, so it is also the city's main orientation area. Eyre Square evolved from common open ground, a market space and park in 1631, to a Victorian Square in the 1830s when it was railed in and enclosed by buildings, to 1960 when it was redeveloped and the railings removed. In 2006, it received an enhancement scheme including upgrad-

Eyre Square

ing the paved northern civic square, the pedestrianisation of the western side of the square, terraced lawns and an eastern enclosed garden/playground area. In general, and despite the controversy surrounding it, the works have been successful with the exception of the quality of finish to the kiosk buildings. The square acts as a meeting place and amenity area for the city, with occasional, multi-functional usage such as concerts, circuses, a Christmas fair and other large public gathering events. It still retains a number of political, urban and maritime memorials, including the John F. Kennedy bust, Liam Mellow's statue, Browne's Doorway and the Quincentennial Fountain. Sadly, in recent years it has lost its most beloved memorial to the City Museum, that of Padraig O'Conaire's life-size statue, which had become one of the iconic features of the square.

Shop Street Area

If Eyre Square is the heart of the city, then the pedestrian spine of the medieval core including Williamgate Street, Shop Street, High Street and Quay Street is the pulsating blood vein. It is here all the energy and

Shop Street

intensity of the city is funnelled down its narrow historic main street, with its layers from the medieval to the modern, a place to shop, meet, entertain, watch and be watched. Starting in Williamgate Street, corresponding with the medieval Great Gate entrance to the city, it follows an organic slightly curved, meandering route, linking with side pedestrian lanes and alleyways and providing a series of small incidental areas for street entertainment. At the centre of the route, it connects with Abbeygate Street Upper and Lower, the main crossroads of the medieval city. At the end of Shop Street it forks into three streets, leading to the three keys elements of the medieval town, Church Yard Street, containing St. Nicholas's Church, Mainguard Street, containing the medieval market area and High Street/Quay Street leading to the medieval port. High Street and Quay Street are now the Latin Quarter, containing most of the pubs and restaurants of the city and the focus of its evening activity and nightlife. The pedestrian area's sole memorial, that of the seated Oscar Wilde and his brother Edward, is both inappropriate and contrived given their tenuous links with the city. The overall route, however, remains the epicentre of Galway's own perception of it sense of place.

The Fishmarket

Originally the site of the medieval port of the city, its current name dates back to the nineteenth century, when the quay was filled in and it be-

came a busy market area for women of the Claddagh area who sold fish from reed baskets to the city's population. Today it is an amenity, leisure and recreational area at the River Corrib estuary edge, a place to sit, relax, take a breath and enjoy the open vista of the river and bay area. If Eyre Square is the heart,

The Fishmarket

Shop Street the blood vein, then the Fishmarket is the lung, a place to exhale the energy of the city inhaled on the journey through the medieval main street. The area is also the starting point for the riverside walk along the Long Walk to the south and as far as the Salmon Weir Bridge to the north. The Fishmarket is also the cultural centre of the city containing the Spanish Arch, City Museum and Blake's Castle, and adjacent to the Druid Theatre, Red Earl Hall and Cultural Cinema. Similar to Eyre Square, it is also the main point of arrival into the city for those travelling from the west over Wolfe Tone Bridge. It contains two memorials, a monument to Christopher Columbus and to mariners lost at sea, reflecting its history as the location of the medieval port.

The Docks

Galway harbour is the city's most immediate connection to the sea and its most visible symbol of its maritime past. It is a busy, bustling place where shipping, boating, fishing, residential, commercial and industrial uses all coexist around the attractive horseshoe amenity form of the port waters. Because of its intimacy as a harbour, it is a popular place for ship spotting,

The Docks

Woodquay

boat watching and just casual browsing. Its waters, amenity and nautical atmosphere make it the most distinguishing place within the city, with strong cultural associations with the historic, medieval centre.

Woodquay

Woodquay is a smaller scale part of the city, centred on a widened street area, which was used traditionally for market purposes. It has more of a feel of a small town than a city, because of the modest, low-key nature of the buildings, uses and activity. It also has a local Galway presence about it, where the shops and pubs are primarily used by residents and local rural people, rather than the visitors to the city.

Waterside

Anchored by the Courthouse and Town Hall Theatre, the Waterside area, as its name suggests, is focused on the River Corrib and in particular the weir area. It remains a quiet retreat from the bustle of the city and where the dominant sound is the surge of the Corrib waters over its weir. Mainly

Waterside

consisting of offices and houses, the Waterfront route from the Salmon Weir Bridge to Eglington Pier, which is the lake harbour, is one of the most attractive and tranquil parts of the city.

The Claddagh

Whilst the traditional fishing village and customs no longer exist, the place name, memories and family connections still do, so it still maintains a strong cultural identity in the city, symbolised today by its distinctive artisan cottages and row housing. It is now a very desirable place to live because of its walking proximity to the city and the great amenity that the Claddagh Basin, river estuary and South Park provides for its inhabitants. Whilst outsiders to the area are no longer referred to as 'transplanters', the Claddagh, along with Shantalla and Bohermore areas, remain the only places where the real Galway accent is still evident.

The Claddagh

Waterways Area

This area lies between the west bank of the River Corrib and the Eglington Canal, consisting of a sinuous series of waterways between which is a terraced housing area, punctuated with other incidental uses such as a church, school, offices and occasional local shops. It is generally a quiet residential place with a calm presence, with narrow streets, no busy traf-

Waterways Area

The West

fic routes and a strong identity and character, shaped by the system of waterways and defined by a simple streetscape network. It remains one of the most pleasant and accessible, habitable areas close to the city centre.

The West

Stretching from the commercial streets of Dominick Street and William Street, which are gradually establishing themselves as the new, alternative left bank area of the city, to the elegant residential area at the Crescent, this is very much a local place within the overall city. There is a great contrast between the cafe culture of Upper Dominick Street, the night-time scene of Lower Dominick Street, the haphazard mix of William Street, and the varied streetscape of Sea Road to the classic formality of the Crescent, on the relatively local route into the city, from the west.

Salthill

From its predominance as a holiday resort, Salthill is now more of a local village serving the surrounding housing areas. It is a bustling centre of

Salthill

activity all year round, with the main busy shopping street opening onto and contrasting with the more sedate nature of the seafront. It still contains memories of its former status as a tourist spot and remains the only traditional shopping village in the city outside the city centre. Besides the shopping, the attraction of Galway Bay and the promenade is still the primary amenity attraction of the area and defines its sense of place.

National University of Ireland, Galway

NUIG is a very distinctive place within the city, with a population of 20,000 and close to the city centre, but remains largely unknown to Galway's general public, outside of staff and students. The campus has incrementally expanded from its original size of 15 hectares in 1845 to over 100 hectares today, occupying an attractive, linear parkland between the west bank of the River Corrib and Newcastle Road. The campus buildings have also increased gradually from the original Quadrangle building and, similar to the rest of the city, the expansion has been more dramatic in the last fifty years, and particularly accelerated in the last twenty years,

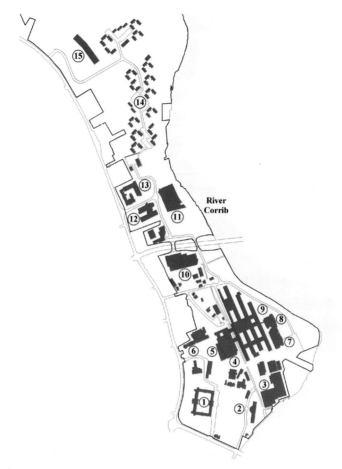

NUI Galway campus and main buildings

with a diverse range of new faculty buildings. The university contains five colleges, consisting of the College of Arts, Social Science and Celtic Studies, College of Business, Public Policy and Law, College of Engineering and Information, College of Medicine, Nursing and Health Services and the College of Science. The various colleges are represented within the campus by a variety of building types and styles, designed by both national and international architects, making it a veritable architectural laboratory for the exploration of design trends and ideas. Because of its piecemeal growth the college has a more organic than coherent feel to it, and the buildings illustrated are the principle faculty structures constructed or under construction in the last forty years.

1. Quadrangle Building

2. Marine Science Institute

3. Student Centre

4. James Hardiman Library

5. Arts, Humanities & Social Science

6. Arts Millennium Building

7. Orbsen Building

8. Information Technology Building

9. Arts Science Building

10. Sports Building

11. School of Engineering

12. School of Nursing

13. School of Business & Economics

14. Corrib Village

15. Bio-Science Research Building

NUI Galway buildings

ARTS AND CULTURE

In recent years, Galway has been bestowed with the label 'City of Culture'. This image has largely derived from its big name, cultural groups and events, such as the Druid Theatre, Macnas and the Arts Festival, and smaller niche events, such as Cúirt Literary Festival, the Galway Film Fleadh, and the Baboró and Tulca Visual Arts Festivals. In addition, the city is witness to a diverse range of artists and musicians who operate at a more local level.

In the modern era, Galway has increased the number of its cultural facilities, but still has a deficit in its overall cultural infrastructure. Coming from an extremely low base of minimum facilities, thirty years ago, the city gained the Leisureland concert venue, Druid Theatre, Town Hall Theatre, Black Box Theatre and new City Museum in the recent past, which has provided a range of base outlets for the performing arts. However, there is still no suitable big concert venue for large outside acts to perform in the city. In the visual arts, there is no public art gallery to display the municipal art collection or temporary space for local and non-local independent artists, and recently even the two private city centre arts galleries have closed. In the literary area, the library remains too small and unable to provide the range of specialist facilities that contemporary city libraries should offer. Consequently, whilst the provision of performing theatre venues has added to Galway's sense of place, its deficit of visual arts, a large concert venue and a modern library undermines its reputation as a city of culture. To overcome this obstacle, the city has depended on the ingenuity of artists and event organisers to address these challenges. The lack of available arts venues relative to the demand placed by the Arts Festival during a concentrated period of time has required the construction of a temporary 'Big Top' music venue and adaption of other buildings for festival purposes such as St. Nicholas' Church and Galway Cathedral. Utilising long-term vacant shop units with free rent and support by Galway City Council is another example of the traditional creative approach to cultural activity in the city, which in many ways also reinforces its cultural reputation.

While Galway has separately developed in the modern era both a reputation as a social and a cultural city, it is more accurate to describe it

Galway's celebratory life

as a combined social cultural city where both activities intertwine, over-lap and at times fuse. It is difficult at times in Galway to distinguish be-tween its social life and its cultural endeavours because of the nature of their interconnection. The weaving of both has its origins in the organic birth and growth of its cultural life, often planned and plotted in its so-cial hub – the pub and where the aftermath of post-mortem or celebra-tion returned to the same hub. Thus the Druid and Quays pub became one, the Arts Festival and Tigh Neachtain became a pair, and Macnas inhabited most of the rest. The inter-celebratory character of both activi-ties is also determined by its festival calendar, where its now renowned festival tradition often fails to distinguish between hard social and soft culture. Thus Galway Races, Oyster Festival, Comedy Festival and Ses-sion Festival, for example, straddle both definitions and conveniently or deliberately attract both serious and fun-seeking punters. The fusion of the two pursuits is also evident in Galway's music scene where even the most skilled and proficient artists move between concert theatre and pub theatre, often on the same night. This integration of the social and cultural impacts on the perception of Galway's sense of place. It is a city of informal formalities, of casual seriousness, and organic planning. There is little highbrow culture or lowbrow social activities, just a generous mix of the two.

Druid Theatre Company

A good example of former students of NUIG impacting on the city, Druid Theatre Company was founded in 1975 by three former members of the

Druid Theatre at Druid Lane

college drama society and was the first Irish professional theatre company to be established outside Dublin. This pioneering endeavour quickly became a major force in Irish theatre, and later internationally, including winning a number of Tony awards. Druid's international reputation has by association provided Galway with a cultural brand name. The quality of work is characterised by their innovative interpretation of the playwright's work, superb production and direction, combined with strong acting. Their original approach grew out of their home theatre, based in Druid Lane, a medieval lane appropriately renamed after the company, consisting of a converted warehouse donated by a local business family. This intimate theatre, where the 'stage' doubles as an audience circulating area, has no traditional backstage area and for some productions the actors construct the stage set as part of the prequel to the drama. They also occasionally engage in asides with the public during, but separate, from the drama, blurring the distinction between audience and actor, real life and stage, reality and fantasy.

Galway Arts Festival

Founded in 1978, the annual Arts Festival provides a fortnightly celebration of cultural activity every July, and is now Ireland's most influential arts festival and a key event in the European arts calendar with a reputation for quality and innovation. Its leading position on the national and international stage has provided Galway with its second cultural brand. The festival concentrates on the performing and visual arts, attracting a range of performers, musicians, artists and writers, creating diverse theatre, music, comedy, art, spectacle and literature. It is a significant outlet for both national and international artists, providing exposure for their work, allowing local and visiting audiences to experience a diversity of leading exponents in their various fields. Besides establishing Galway as one of the leading centres for the arts in Ireland, with a reputation for cultural excellence, the festival attracts 150,000 visitors annually and is a major contributor to the city's celebratory activities and, consequently, a key element in its sense of place.

Galway Arts Festival Big Top

Macnas

In its originality, Macnas is the Druid brought outdoors. Established in 1986 and influenced by the Spanish Catalan performance group Els Commediants, who performed in the Galway Arts festival in 1985, Macnas, which translates from the Irish as 'joyful abandonment', completes the trio of Galway's iconic cultural brands. Echoing the indoor Taibhdhearc, the Irish-speaking theatre which means 'behold the spectacle', and with strong, original roots in the bilingual aspect of the city, the street performance company always lives up to its name with a mixture of colour, spectacle and exuberance. In a city whose only previous experience of parades was the annual, formal and staid St. Patrick's Day Parade in the cold of March, Macnas brings a riot of energy, theatre and anarchy in the heat of summer. Their performances, which tend to be theme-based, attract enormous expectant crowds to the streets of the city during the Arts Festival and have influenced and changed the nature of parade activity in Ireland. The company has performed in over twenty countries

Macnas parade through the streets of Galway

The Galway Races

worldwide, advancing Galway's reputation as a cradle of culture. Their community-based ethos continues to provide numerous young people with their theatrical debut on the street stage of Galway City.

Galway Races

The Galway Races, started in 1869, is not only the biggest and longest horse racing festival in Ireland, it is now one of the world's main race meetings, attracting over 150,000 spectators annually. A subject of a poem by W.B. Yeats and popularised in folk songs by the Clancy Brothers and the Chieftains, its importance today is highlighted by the national television station covering the week long race meeting live, including all its social trappings, which again confirms Galway's image as a social event centre. Starting on the last Monday of July each year, the Galway Races echo pagan festivals of old, marking the transition from summer to autumn, the start of both the farmers' and builders' holidays and an unofficial week-long holiday for the city. The race meeting is essentially a large outdoor party for all age groups and categories, where the horse racing is often incidental, despite the extensive betting based on 'a good tip'. The race course itself measures over one mile, mirroring the historical fortunes of the city by starting on the high part of the course, before going into a steep decline in the middle and a sharp incline to the finish line. Whilst the festival event is located in the eastern suburbs of the city, the party quickly transfers after the daily race meeting into the city centre for the 'Mardi Gras' nightly celebrations.

Galway Maritime Festivals

The tri-annual Volvo Round the World Ocean Race and the Annual Galway International Oyster Festival provide the perfect marriage of Galway's historic maritime tradition with the contemporary festival tradition as each exploits Galway's traditional association with the sea. The Volvo Ocean Race, which had a stopover stage in Galway in 2009 and the finishing stage in 2012, was the biggest and most successful festival event hosted in the city. The 2009 festival had final attendance figures of 650,000 with the 2012 event estimated at 750,000. Similar to the Galway

Volvo Ocean Race in Galway Harbour

Races, where the actual race is almost incidental to the overall carnival atmosphere and numerous fringe activities, it has a cross sectional appeal, attracting young and old, singles and families, sailors and non-sailors, local, national and international visitors. Galway is the smallest city ever to host the finishing stage, across all the world cities that compete for the prestigious event, which demonstrates the success and impact of the 2009 stopover stage, enhanced by the intimacy and immediacy of Galway harbour.

The Galway Oyster Festival, held in the last weekend of September, is the world's longest running international oyster festival, launched in 1954. It attracts 10,000 visitors to the city each year for that unique cocktail of seafood, champagne and Guinness. The high point of the event is the World Oyster Opening Competition, where champions aim to open thirty oysters in less than two minutes.

Sporting Galway

There is a diverse sporting tradition in Galway, ranging from the most popular, including Gaelic games, soccer and rugby, to the more niche sports of horse and greyhound racing, rowing, golf and motorsport. Pearse Stadium in Salthill is the home venue for both Galway's senior Gaelic football and hurling teams, where spectators to both games get a unique opportunity to enjoy a Gaelic match in a resort setting. Besides the local clubs, the Gaelic tradition in Galway is generally divided on a line extending out from the city with hurling confined to the south of the county and football to the north. In comparison to Gaelic games which continues over the summer season, both rugby and soccer generally run through the winter season. Galway has two senior soccer clubs playing in the League of Ireland, following the recent demise of Galway United, who were based in Terryland Park – Salthill Devon located in Drum and Mervue United based in Mervue. At local level, the game has a large involvement and participation throughout the city, and in 2012 lost its most renowned player, Eamon 'Chick' Deacy, who won both England and European honours in the 1980s. Rugby also has an extensive popularity in the city and contains two senior teams competing in All Ireland League competitions, Galwegians and Corinthians. The Connacht Rugby Team,

Hurling match at Pearse Stadium

who play in both the Magners League and the Heineken Cup, has their home base in the city – at the College Showgrounds, a location they share with the Greyhound Racing track. It has been argued that the amalgamation of the major clubs in both soccer and rugby codes into one city club would make them more competitive at an all Ireland level. However, local tradition, history and identity are stronger forces than possible advancement on the national stage. Overall, while sport in Galway tends to receive a smaller billing than the more illustrious image of its cultural and festival tradition, it has a far greater and more widespread participation across the city than its more renowned big ticket events.

OTHER ELEMENTS OF GALWAY'S SENSE OF PLACE

O nce you move outside the orbit of the typical understanding of Galway's sense of place, which is the natural and built environment of the city, the other ingredients that contribute to its makeup are less visible. However, the physical city should only be seen as the stage set in which the everyday drama of the city is acted out. That sense of theatre in the city is a major contributor to its sense of place – for some, it is the prime contributor. These living elements are varied and diverse, connected in a loose, informal way. Their main themes and patterns lie in the social and cultural celebratory life of the city, which provide the context for utilising and amplifying the physical city. Most of the elements remain rooted in the city, creating a reference for its inhabitants and a memory for visitors.

University Life

The two third level colleges, NUIG and GMIT, make a fundamental contribution to Galway's sense of place. That contribution is not just the physical campus areas of both institutions, which are outside the general experience of the citizens and visitors to the city, but in the student body. NUIG with 17,000 students and GMIT with 8,000 students, account for one-third of Galway's total population of 75,000. This percentage is extremely high by Irish city standards and is the main reason that Galway exudes a feeling of youthful and sometimes over exuberant energy. NUIG in particular, because of its close proximity to the city centre, has always had a close association with the city and its student population see the town as their common room. Much of the affinity that students have for Galway, once in Galway, manifests itself in an elastic stretching of their student life to prolong their studies of both their chosen subject and city. It also emerges in the number of former students who continue to reside in the city and contribute to its economic, cultural and social life.

Pubs and Traditional Music

For a lot of locals and visitors, Galway's sense of place is embodied in its pubs – urban retreats where people meet, drink and chat earnestly, frivolously or incoherently. Galway pubs come in all variations and hues, each having their own particular mix of customers. The best ones combine the vital ingredients of character, conviviality and banter, where age, status or origin are irrelevant. They vary from quiet hideaways to noisy theatres, from contemplation to debate and from music sessions to drinking sessions. Most of the pubs form part of the city streetscape. The exception and the oldest pub in Galway, Tigh Neachtains, occupies a prominent position on the corner of Quay Street and Cross Street. Dating back to the nineteenth century, the pub was originally the eighteenth century townhouse of Richard Martin, or Humanity Dick, a member of one of Galway's Tribe families who owned the largest Irish estate in Connemara. The pub, which has been in the family for three generations, is popular with literary and music types, attracts both locals and visitors and has what Myles na gCopaleen described as the essential ingredient in a pub – a sense of permanence. The original layout is still intact, consisting of alcoves, snugs and long room, including a separate counter from when the pub doubled as a shop, behind which customers can now imbibe, blurring the traditional boundary between publican and punter. The pub sells both its own distinctive single malts and the local Galway Hooker pale ale.

Tigh Neachtains Pub

Galway has a deserved reputation as being a centre for Irish traditional music. Some of the leading exponents in the field are closely associated with the city including Frankie Gavin, Sharon Shannon, Martin O'Connor, Ringo McDonagh, Dolores Keane and Alec Finn. Galway is the spiritual home of the renowned traditional group De Danann and a lot of its pubs provide both formal and informal music sessions. Regular traditional sessions are held in the Crane Bar, Cookes Thatched Pub and Monroe's, while spontaneous sessions can be heard in Taffes, Tigh Coili and Tigh Neachtains. For a lot of visitors to the city, a traditional music session in one of its atmospheric pub settings is sufficient to define Galway's sense of place.

Legendary traditional musician Frankie Gavin

117

Pubs of Galway

Pedestrianisation

The pedestrianisation programme within the city centre was the single most important development in the twenty-five year span of urban renewal, and arguably in the whole fifty-year modern era. With pedestrianisation the city's historic core was reclaimed, exposing the charm and richness of the city and contributing enormously to the quality of urban life. The extension of the pedestrian initiative to create the riverside and canal walks has emphasised water as the defining feature of the city. Citizens and visitors can now rejoice in the pedestrian zone of the city, where the rhythm, routine and rituals of city life can be observed. The pedestrian fabric of spaces is ideal for the city explorer, both visitors and locals alike, who equally enjoy the intimate scale of enclosure, the absence of road traffic and the concentration of activity in small spaces.

The pedestrian spaces provide numerous niches for street performers and for casual gathering, meeting friends, hanging out, people watching and general spontaneity. It has proved ideal for festival and celebratory events, catering for outdoor markets, including the weekly organic market, food market, art market and craft market. Surprisingly, it has encouraged a culture of outdoor cafes and dining, as well as outdoor pubs. In essence, pedestrianisation has supported exchange – the exchange of goods, money and services, the exchange of glances, greetings and conversation, the exchange of music, theatre and spectacle. The pedestrian area is now the primary place of identity for the city and the focus for both its tourists and inhabitants.

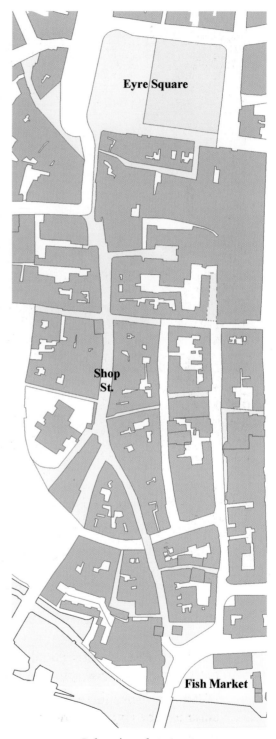

Galway's pedestrian zone

Street culture in the Latin Quarter of Quay Street

Street Culture

The pedestrianisation of the city's main spine has become the stage for street entertainment and an outdoor extension of its pubs and restaurants. The street entertainment involves a bewildering range of buskers, artists, exhibitionists and street theatre including musicians, singers, mime artists, fire eaters, cartoonists, jugglers, high wire artists, hair braiders, face painters and balloon artists, all competing for the ten favourite vantage points along the street to entertain, and be sustained by, the constant flow of people. The street culture extends down into High Street and Quay Street, where the pub drinkers have vacated the bar counter and diners their indoor tables for a bout of al-fresco drinking and dining, a sight regarded as previously unimaginable in the wet and often windy climate of Galway. However, natural curiosity, increased potential for people watching and chance encounters have obviously compensated for the climate, and the extensive canopy

*Street artist (above) and street
performer (right)*

covering over the outdoor seating
is provided to reduce the impact
of rain rather than protection from
the sun. This very recent development of Galway's street culture has
brought a whole new dimension to
the city, involving the public using
the streetscape for uses other than
solely as a route, which both further reveals and enhances its sense
of belonging, ownership and place
– a Mediterranean feeling, though
without the weather.

Galwegians of Note

According to the latest census, half of the population of Galway were born outside the city or country and a quarter were born outside the state, which makes Galway the most cosmopolitan and international city in Ireland. Otherwise, in a city with such a high transitory population, increased importance is given to native or local people in creating a stable reference point for its inhabitants and to ground its sense of place. Local people create the rock and anchor, around which the visiting population can orbit. The value of the native population lies in their participation, rather than just the mere observation, of the city, thus creating a city society made up of a cluster of communities. That cluster of communities is not solely defined by city districts or neighbourhoods, but also by family, school, worship, work, sport and social communities. Citizens of the city can often straddle all community types, but the core component of any of the communities is the individual. Thus, while Galway's base structure can be said to be made up of families and districts, it is the single individual that for many people defines the Galwayness of the place. These individuals come in all ages, categories and functions, but they share a common meaning – they are all associated with and are representative of the city. This association can cover all fields from those with a national profile, to a local profile, to just a personal contact. It can range from knowing them, observing them, to being just aware of them. Their activities can be simple, functional or elaborate. Their contribution to the fabric of Galway society and its sense of place is one of belonging, connection or participation.

Galway's currently best known personality is Ireland's first citizen, Michael D. Higgins, elected President of Ireland in 2011. Despite his roots in both Limerick and Clare, he is more associated with Galway City, having studied in University College Galway, where he was later to lecture in Political Science and Sociology. One of the few people in Ireland known solely by his first name and middle initial, Michael D. with the 'D' providing the distinguishing mark in a country full of Michaels, his life both contrasts and reflects the City of the Tribes, where he has lived for most of his life. Following his first attempt in 1969, he eventually succeeded in 1981 to being elected as a Labour TD for Galway in a city traditionally

Padraic Breathnach, Actor

Garry Hynes, Druid Theatre Company

Pat McDonagh, Businessman

Sharon Shannon, Musician

President Michael D. Higgins

Rita Ann Higgins, Poet

Ollie Jennings, Sawdoctors Manager

Mayor Hildegarde Naughton

Tommy Tiernan, Comedian

Mary Coughlan, Singer

Tom Kenny, Kenny's Bookshop

Maire Geoghegan Quinn, EU Commisioner

Some well known people of Galway

dominated by more right of centre parties. He continued to be TD until elected as President and twice served as Mayor of Galway in 1982/83 and 1991/92. His period as Minister for Arts, Culture and the Gaeltacht in the 1993/97 government echoed his own personal interests outside of politics – that of a poet, writer and fluent speaker in both the English and Irish language – and that of his native city with its cultural and bilingual credentials. His record on human rights is also in tune with the city's

Lady Gregory

sense of a questioning and alternate viewpoint. Following in the footsteps of the two highly regarded previous Presidents, Michael D. brings his own unique mix of intellect and sociability, highlighter and advocate of social values, combined with a mastery and delivery of language.

In a previous historical era Lady Gregory featured prominently in the social and cultural life of the city. Born Isabella Augusta Persee, she came from the well known Anglo Irish Persee family, who had a major impact on the city during the nineteenth century. The family city residence was at 47 Dominick Street, currently the Galway Arts Centre, and the family dynasty had numerous distillery and mill businesses in the city during that period. Later, as Lady Gregory, she was an influential dramatist and folklorist, and had a profound impact on the Irish Literary Revival. She co-founded the Abbey Theatre in Dublin with W.B. Yeats with whom she had a lifelong friendship and acted as a mentor to some notable writers such as J.M. Synge, Sean O'Casey and George Bernard Shaw who described her as 'the greatest living Irishwoman'.

Directly across the river from Lady Gregory's city home, another woman from the other side of the social divide was to make an impact on Irish literature in a different guise around the same period. Reared at

Number 4 Bowling Green, Nora Barnacle, as an 18-year-old, was to have her first romantic encounter with Ireland's world famous writer, James Joyce on June 16, 1904, a date later chosen as the setting for his greatest novel *Ulysses* and to become known and celebrated as 'Bloomsday'. They emigrated to continental Europe where they later married and lived in Austria, France and Switzerland. They had two children and, following Joyce's death in 1941, Nora lived in Zurich where she died in 1951.

Down river from Nora's childhood home, Galway's best loved literary figure emerged from the maritime setting of the Docks. Padraig O'Conaire, born on Dock Road, was later to be regarded as the most influential Irish language storywriter of the early twentieth century. Involved in the Gaelic League and a pioneer in the Irish Literary Revival, his best known short stories include 'Mascal Beag Dubh' and 'Nora Mharcais Bhig'. Following his death, a life-size statue in his honour was erected in Eyre Square in 1935 which was recently relocated to the City Museum.

Nora Barnacle's home

Upriver from O'Conaire's birthplace, another local writer of renown was reared at Waterside. Born in 1915, Walter Macken's interest in the arts started as an actor in the local Irish language theatre – the Taibhdhearc. He later became better known as a writer of short stories, novels and plays. His best known books include *Rain on the Wind*, *Seek the Fair Land* and *The Silent People*. Macken died in 1967.

Today, Galway's literary tradition is continued through the writings of, among others, Ken Bruen, a native writer of modern crime fiction and thrillers. Best known for his award winning Jack Taylor series of novels, which follows the life of an erratic private investigator. Interestingly, the series also charts the social changes in Galway resulting from Celtic Tiger Ireland of the post-1990s.

Visitors

Galway is a city of locals and visitors, with the visitors often outnumbering the locals at particular times of the year, attracted to its educational, shopping, cultural, social or just casual activities. The visitors are not a homogenous grouping, but come under a diverse range of types, covering origin, purpose, age and duration of stay. In broad terms, this community of strangers include the transient tourist population, both national and international, the seasonal student body, the regional shopping visitors and the daytime working community. When this is combined with the permanent resident population, it provides for a rich and varied cultural mix, which creates the cosmopolitan atmosphere of Galway and is a key generator of its vibrancy, dynamism and energy. This body of visiting humanity also borrows, as well as contributes to, its sense of place, providing the irony of being a large part of the story and experience that they seek. For the resident population, the diversity of visitors is not always detectable, except when there is an obvious accent, look or intent.

For the detectable visitors, they all represent something subliminally for the city's inhabitants, which reconciles the sharing of its sense of place. Consequently, the student body represent the freedom and challenge of youth, the European visitor recalls Galway's strong maritime link with Europe, the American visitors symbolise the strong post-Famine Galway/America connection, and the domestic visitor reflects Salthill's traditional attraction as a native holiday choice. Some visitors of international stature can raise the profile of Galway worldwide, creating a certain image of the city. The visits of Presidents John F. Kennedy in 1963 and Ronald Reagan in 1984, and the arrival of Pope John Paul in 1979, established Galway as a city of importance. Ironically, the Youth Mass for the Pope's visit did more to reinforce the image of Galway as a young, party-loving city than the renewal of the Church in the city. Galway's reputation for warmth and friendliness in receiving visitors was noted in ongoing official documentation as far back as 1538. Overall, Galway's sea port trading status and history always militated against the city developing

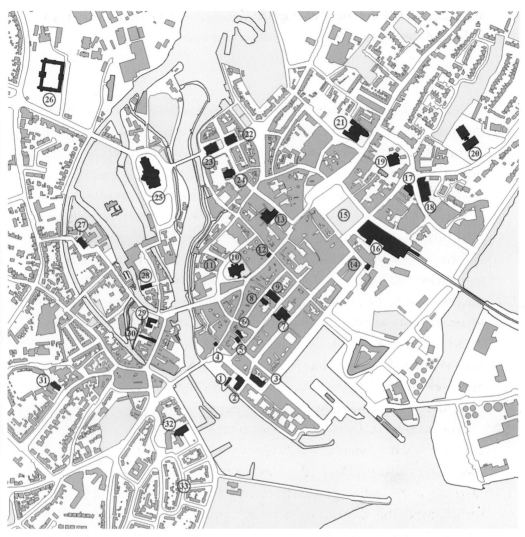

1. Spanish Arch
2. City Museum
3. Art House Cinema
4. Blake's Castle
5. Red Earl's Hall
6. Druid Theatre
7. City Library
8. Taibhdhearc Theatre
9. Augustine Church
10. St. Nicholas' Church
11. Nora Barnacle's House

12. Lynch's Castle
13. General Post Office
14. Methodist Church
15. Eyre Square
16. RailwayStation/
    Meyrick Hotel
17. Tourist Office
18. Bus Station
19. St. Patrick's Church
20. Galway City Council
21. Galway County Council
22. Town Hall Theatre

23. Court House
24. Franciscan Church
25. Galway Cathedral
26. NUIG
27. St. Joseph's Church
28. Nun's Island Theatre
29. Garda Station
30. Galway Arts Centre
31. St. Ignatius' Church
32. Dominican Church
33. The Claddagh

Galway City visitor attractions and public buildings

an insular personality, and ensured an outward open-mindedness which exists today in the acceptance of visitors to the city.

Saturday Market

Galway was built primarily for market purposes which developed into a regionally significant trading city, but even during the nineteenth century the market was still the predominant method and place for the buying and selling of goods, mainly farm produce. Galway had numerous distinctive, specialist markets associated with particular places such as a hay market, potato market, fish market, turf market, pig market, cattle market, horse market, meat market, bread market, vegetable market, corn market and butter market. The Saturday market on Church Yard Street next to St. Nicholas' Church continues that tradition, which turned often banal and mundane city spaces into vibrant and exciting places of public life. The outdoor Saturday market, which sells farm produce, vegetables and fruit, craftwork, hot food, books and artwork, is an intimate, bustling affair with the narrowness of the market street and the informality of its larger, open market area giving a meandering, jumble

The two main surviving features of medieval Galway, St Nicholas' Church and the Saturday Market – still catering for the body and soul of its citizens

Cait Curran

Paddy Hogan

Kate Zyderlaan

Daniel Rosen

Jeannette Kochen

Mike Silke

Lisa King

Bernie Gunning

Jane O' Sullivan

Dirk Flake

Cobi Denheyer

Paul Illien

ST. NICHOLAS'
CHURCH

CHURCH
YARD
STREET

LOMBARD STREET

Saturday Market layout and well known stall holders

feel to it, ideal for both serious as well as casual browsing and bargaining. There is a great continuity in the market, not just in the continuance of a long tradition that started in the late medieval period, but in the market producers themselves, many of whom have been selling from the same stall location for years. Overall, the Galway outdoor Saturday market is a wonderful celebration of the local food and craft sectors and a vital part of Galway's sense of place.

Eyre Square Fountain

Designed by the recently deceased sculptor Eamon O'Doherty, responsible for many public sculptures in Ireland, as a result of a competition to commemorate the 1984 Quincentennial Celebrations, the fountain has taken over from the recently removed Padraig O'Conaire statue as being the iconic feature of Eyre Square. Constructed in rusted corten steel, this simple but evocative sculpture reflects Galway's maritime history, in particular the distinctive brown sails of the famous Galway Hooker fishing boats, which are captured and echoed in a stylized form. The fountain remains the most impressive public monument in the city and one which is most representative of the city's origin and evolution.

Eyre Square Fountain

Lanes and Alleys

The medieval city founded by the Normans consisted of fourteen streets and fourteen lanes and alleys within the city walls. Most of the lanes and alleys still remain intact, and today are now all pedestrianised, which helps in giving a sense of their original medieval usage. Some of the names still remain, reflecting their function or association, such as Ball Alley Lane, Kirwan's Lane, Barrack lane, Church Lane and Buttermilk Lane. They still serve the function of interconnecting the main streets and providing shortcuts as one moves around and through the city centre. They resonate with the status of containing the humble, commonplace houses of the medieval town and the hierarchal nature of the city

Buttermilk Walk

structure and form. In many ways, their use today has elevated their position in the lower order and importance in the city.

Quirks and Features

Throughout the city centre there are some subtle but notable features and quirks in the general streetscape which on their own are unremarkable, but collectively provide Galway with a pattern of distinguishing oddity and uniqueness. The first feature is the rounded corner which was a nineteenth century trend in many of Galway's corner buildings, contrasting

Rounded corners

Decorated building on Shop Street

Street art on Quay Street

with the sharp corner pattern of the earlier medieval footprint. These corners range from shops to houses and many incorporate an entrance into the curve. The second quirk is the occasional example of hidden or partially hidden buildings or parts of buildings in the townscape caused by particular odd aspects of ownership and property boundaries. Finally, there are a number of buildings which are part of the streetscape, but because of their particular design or decoration announce themselves in a very personal way and have become part of the quirks of its townscape.

Local Shops

The city centre's main function as a shopping area is reflected in both the range and variety of shops in terms of type, size and character. These shops represent the values and aspirations of their time and generation. Consequently, shops are constantly renewing, extending or changing in terms of ownership, use and style. Shops in the city can be broadly divided into two categories – the smaller, indigenous shop owned and operated by local people and the larger national or foreign multiple, brand names, mainly owned and managed by outside companies. With the ever expanding city and increased tourism, the nature of shopping is also changing from the local to the non-local, leading to a gradual shift in the character of the shopping experience. Galway is slowly moving to the uniform, universal model of cities with similar shops, brand names and choice. This is the nature of growth and change in all modern cities. However, Galway still retains a considerable stock of indigenous shops, which are part of both the memory and sense of place of the city. In time, and generally over a period of a generation, the new arrivals to the city shopping experience will also become part of that memory and place.

The Craic

If Temple Bar in Dublin is the focus for international visitors seeking fun, then Galway would appear to be the national destination for the Gaelic equivalent – the craic. While craic is generally seen as fun, enjoyment and having a good time, it can deviate between two extremes. Technically translated from Gaelic it means 'conversation and chat' in its most polite translation, or 'cracked crazy person' in its more exuberant meaning.

Never to be confused with the international meaning of the word crack, referring to narcotics, nevertheless Galway craic can induce a similar high, albeit a natural one. The craic in Galway generally revolves around its pub culture, with Galway Race week being the high point of the annual programme. Indeed for years, the Galway Races boasted about having the longest bar in the world and, consequently, ensuring the best craic. In general, the craic is a weekend pursuit, best enjoyed when it just happens rather than planned. Spontaneity rather than forced organisation is

Shops of Galway

the key and where events are allowed to take their own shape. It also has a seasonal dimension. Christmas reunions are an annual source of craic in Galway, while the St. Patrick's Day celebrations often eventually reveal the cracks in craic. The Macnas parade is normally a good prequel to craic with an international dimension, where the street carnival often induces foreigners to chase craic as seriously as the Irish. Of course, Galway has a history in this activity. Particularly during the puritanical Protestant era, the Gaelic Irish rebelled against the new social order and cultivated more expressive endeavours. Thus the tradition of 'Maying in Menlo', a festive period of merriment, games, sports, gambling, socialising and drinking, was popular in the city in the eighteenth and nineteenth centuries with possible origins in medieval times. Nude bathing was also a source of concern for the ruling class, although again it would appear to be a form of rebellion or poverty rather than an activity suitable to Galway's climate. While craic can hardly define a sense of place, the pursuit of craic in Galway is a local and national hobby, vigorously undertaken, and the city is now clearly identified with this enjoyable pastime. Less a sense of place, more a place of sense and nonsense.

City of Commerce

Galway, like all cities, and despite its social and cultural reputation, is at its core a city of commerce. The city itself was founded by the Norman for the purpose of profit and its whole evolution and growth from then was shaped by its economic fortunes. Its history of prosperity, stagnation or decline was directly linked to its market activities and the bottom line of profit and loss. Even its benevolent nickname, 'the Tribes of Galway', derived from the astute business-minded merchant families, was guided by the twin pursuits of wealth and power. Today, its traditional market stature has morphed into a more complex commerciality with diverse categories including retail, manufacturing, tourism and office-based businesses, but still essentially a trading city of goods and services. Its commercial life underpins and anchors its more popular image, that of its social cultural life, which itself is also part of its commerciality. Thus, the numerous social and cultural festivals, whilst promoted under the banner of arts and culture, are usually defined more by how much they

City of commerce

are worth to the local economy than by their artistic merit. Whilst this may seem like a crass and mercenary approach, it does reveal the commercial essence at the core of the city, without which the city would not exist and would not survive.

Galway's fiscal status also impacts on its sense of place. Prosperity and impoverishment bring two totally different moods to the city. Most commentary on the city, up to the modern era, described the sense of poverty and dereliction which pervaded the city up to the 1960s. In contrast, the air of prosperity since then has helped redefine its sense of place. Crucially, that commercial prosperity has facilitated the evolution and growth of all of the other city ancillary activities, which now define its present day image.

Galway Tiger

Ireland's boom to bust story has been well told at this stage, involving acres of print and hours of air time, confirming that the nation is better at recording and recounting things than predicting them. The general consensus is of corporate, regulatory and political systems failure caused by greed, recklessness and incompetence, all part of the human condition, in a society where the line between greed and profit, recklessness and enterprise, incompetence and ability is not defined until there is an outcome. The only questionable benefit so far for the country is the realisation that other peripheral countries in Europe with very different histories to Ireland's are also in the same boat, confirming that Ireland can now officially stop blaming the Famine and a colonial past for its national character flaws.

During that era, Galway followed a similar pattern as the nationwide Celtic roar, where land and property prices surged. Over that period, apartments halved in area but quadrupled in price and a weekly newspaper column of comparative property prices never quite explained why a modest terraced house in the city was more valuable than a villa in France, perhaps because nobody asked or wanted to know. Like all property bubbles, it was accompanied by a psychological bubble where people became hermetically sealed from reality and common sense.

All areas had their symbols of that era of consumption. For Galway, the most potent symbol was during the Galway Races, notable for its attraction for ordinary people. That symbol was not, ironically, the presence of the infamous 'Galway Tent' (a corporate fundraiser for Fianna Fáil, then Ireland's biggest political party) but the sight of a flock of helicopters ferrying overly busy race-goers from the city centre to the race meeting. As a symbol, the helicopter revealed everything about that period – noisy, conspicuous, aloof, incongruous, ungrounded, carried away. The helicopters are now gone, but they have left a trail. Galway has few of the visible signs of abandoned developments or unsold houses, although there is a large overhang of apartments and sites bought at inflated prices. This is due to Galway's traditional high site and land costs which over that period increased exponentially, forcing smaller operators to outlying provincial towns and encouraging larger ones to the Greater Dublin area.

The residue, however, which may impact on Galway's future in maintaining its sense of place, is the possibility of social changes, that is, the lack of mobility for existing home owners and perhaps the increased perception of risk attached to property investment.

IMAGE AND SUBSTANCE, MYTH AND REALITY

Galway is characterised by its own local variety of complexities, contrasts and contradictions. It also displays its own native flavour of ambivalence, ambiguities and exaggerations. Consequently, it is difficult at times to distinguish between image and substance, myth and truth, story and illusion, real and imagined. This difficulty is further compounded by the knowledge that some legends may be fact and some historical facts may be fiction, depending on who is recording and interpreting history. A good example is Hardiman's famous *History of Galway* of 1820, where the recording of Mayor Lynch hanging his son at Lynch's Castle for a crime of passion is now regarded as just a good story, albeit well told. This blurring of reality and imagination in Galway has many roots. Galway emerged in the middle of an existing Gaelic tradition, rich in legend and folklore, where storytelling was valued and enjoyed. The creation of an Anglo Irish enclave in an Irish hinterland brought both a clash and a fusion of two cultures, where the settlers had to connive, manipulate and deceive in order to navigate their way through a maze of divided loyalties. The issue of language is also significant where at its birth Gaelic, French and English coalesced in the city and created the experience of misunderstandings, misinterpretations and finally lost meanings in the eventual translation to English. The development of the tourist industry also provided a parallel release of new storytelling and imagination to both entice and entertain the visitor where a good yarn was always better than a bad truth.

Today, some of the fantasy is subtle, at times more overt. Some of the image is self-proclaimed, while the rest is conferred from outside. The result, if not a split or triple personality, then is certainly a flexible one. Does the fact that the city is founded on the three different generic rock types have an impact, or that the bedrock under the city centre is 70 million years older than the west of the city and 120 million years older than the east of the city? The story of it urban myths inevitably must start with the ambiguity surrounding the origins of its name, Galway or *Gaillimh*, an uncertainty which is fairly unique in a county where the easy and accurate sourcing of Gaelic personal names and placenames is a proud tradition. Like an orphan without a known origin or identity, the uncertainty has proved a fertile ground for the imagination, between mythmakers and historians, but has allowed Galway to adopt whichever identity it desires and occasionally re-invent itself to whichever image it seeks. Its place-name ambiguity is matched by its geographical ambiguity, captured in the myth of Galway Bay being originally a lake, known as Loch Lurgan and Lough Corrib, being originally part of the sea from the name *oileann* or 'son of the sea', which raises the spectre of the River Corrib, on whose rock Galway was founded, flowing, contrary to all known patterns, from a sea into a lake.

However, it is in its history of conquest and conflict where there is the clearest pattern. It is evident in the permanent conundrum of the Anglo Irish settlers in Galway, where to the Irish they were English and to the English they were Irish. The fusion of both cultures combined the stereotypical description based on the facial traits of both, which for the native Irish was the ability to turn a blind eye and talk out of both sides of their mouth at the same time, and for the foreign English consisted of bearing a stiff upper lip and their preference for turning up their nose. Of course, for the Gaelic population, it resulted in the proud observation of the English becoming more Irish than the Irish themselves, oblivious to the aspirations of the Irish becoming more English than the English themselves.

Amongst the Anglo Norman families themselves, there was a different dynamic, particularly between the pompous Catholic merchant families and the puritan Protestant ruling class. With their loss of power and authority, which was never official or validated in the first place, the self-appointed merchants dispensed with their pride and resorted to smuggling to maintain their trade and power. Consequently, the image of the merchant princes deviated between the fourteen proud Tribes of Galway, twice as many as the great ancient city of Rome, and that of a medieval mafia where family loyalty and pursuit of wealth reigned supreme. So while the phrase 'as proud as a Galway merchant' was known in Continental Europe, back in Galway the de Burgo Norman founders of the city referred to them as 'petty peddlers and bank route merchants'.

Substance is also relevant to the description of the city. The term 'Medieval City' is somewhat misleading, but understandable. In reality, most of the city core is post-medieval, primarily nineteenth century, but constructed on the original medieval footprint. In addition, the high concentration of sixteenth and seventeenth century houses in the city are often treated as medieval or late medieval, even though in European terms these centuries are described as the Renaissance period. However, because Galway was a late comer to most emerging periods and the European Renaissance style never really extended to Galway, they fit more comfortably in the medieval tradition if not period. So while Galway's medieval credentials are technically tenuous, they have a certain merit, if not purity.

The most Irish of cities is another label frequently attached to Galway. Again, whilst this phrase is visually understandable, it is historically incorrect. Galway, albeit a late starter in urban terms, followed the same pattern of foreign conquest as all the main cities in Ireland. Indeed, relative to Limerick, its nearest comparable-sized city, its evolution was almost identical, with the exception of the early Viking settlement. Where it deviated from Limerick and all the other Irish cities was the absence of city building during the eighteenth century, after the new Protestant order was established nationwide. Due to the lack of wealth of the Protestant settlers, the flight of the merchants, the drift to contraband trading due to high taxes and the general impoverishment of the surrounding Gaelic hinterland, Galway never experienced the Georgian expansion in town planning and construction as did other cities. Consequently, the fact that Galway is built of informal grey local stone rather than formal red colonial brick is attributable to a lack of planter wealth rather than an Irish influence.

Galway is often referred to as a bilingual city and the capital city of the Gaeltacht. It is technically located in a mainly Gaeltacht area where almost fifty per cent of the population claim to speak Irish. NUIG is a designated bilingual university and holds the archive of spoken material for the Celtic languages. However, the instance of the spoken language in the modern city is so rare, and has probably been overtaken by a range of other foreign languages, that its multilingual or bilingual label more accurately refers to the English and Polish languages. The term entrance city to the Gaeltacht is also a more apt description. With the language almost extinct in the city, what is left is tokenism and gestures such as the requirement to have new English-speaking housing areas and new roads in the city named in Irish only, which occupies the same mindset as compulsory Irish for exams and *cupla focail* (the short, obligatory and often rudimentary use of Irish on formal occasions) which does little to promote its suspect bilingual status.

Galway's connection with Spain also has an element of fact and fantasy. Galway certainly traded with Spain during medieval times, but not exclusively so. The Spanish Armada incident may have sparked a greater connection and empathy with Spain than was necessarily the case. It evolved into an identification with Spain which is more curious than credible, and extended to both buildings and people. Thus Galway Cathedral was designed with the presumed Spanish architectural influence on its townscape where none actually existed. The Spanish Arch was named because of some romantic attachment to Spain. In another form of romance, the presence of dark-haired and sallow-skinned natives was Galway's proud boast that it was a very romantic city, which disregarded the possibility that it was the Spanish who were romantic and Galway was just willing.

It is in the tourist sphere, however, that story and fact has its greatest interaction. The fault, if it is a fault, for this flight to imagination can be traced to the middle of the seventeenth century and the famous pictorial map of the city, greatly embellished and exaggerated to present the ideal medieval city. That type of creativity later informed other projects such as the Claddagh Ring, which now appears not to be exclusive to the Claddagh or indeed even Ireland, but with the help of presentations of this official Galway merchandise to both Presidents Kennedy and Reagan helped to seal the myth. The infamous Lynch memorial window is another more blatant example of this illusionary approach. On viewing the window in 1939, the Dublin poet Louis McNeice recounted in his autobiography that 'Galway was the strangest city in Ireland, austerely grey, half the houses ruins, the skull and crossbones, emblem of the Lynch family carved in relief on the walls', either unaware that it was a fake, which made it puzzling, or knowing that it was a fake, which made it even more puzzling.

Perhaps not as strange was the decision of Galway to adopt the nickname 'The Tribesman' from the famous fourteen tribes of the city. The alternative, which was deemed not as palatable but which still evoked the city's maritime and fishing past, and a term used to describe the native Irish, was the phrase 'herring chokers' – perhaps too common and vivid for general consumption and a proud image. It is part of the irony of the city that its adopted nickname of the Tribesmen can be viewed benignly, as representing the golden age of its merchant and trading heritage, or malignantly, as a colonial, imperialist force of oppression and exploitation. (The significance of the number fourteen in medieval Galway is not clear, but it is curious that the medieval walled town had fourteen ramparts, fourteen towers, fourteen streets, fourteen lanes and fourteen tribes.)

Transformation and contradictions are evident in its most well-known buildings and events. St. Nicholas' Cathedral evolved in ecclesiastical confusion, unsure of its Catholic or Protestant status because it oscillated so much between both over the centuries. Galway Cathedral, the most traditional and conservative of edifices, nevertheless carries two portraits from the non-ecclesiastical world, the Irish patriot Padraig Pearse and the US President John F. Kennedy, both however, secular saints of 1960s Ireland. NUIG was denounced by the Irish clergy as the 'Godless College' when founded in 1849 because of its non-denominational status, but proceeded to allow one of its eminent members to become its first president. The Galway Races was first founded by the elite and privileged members of the Protestant landlord class, and yet today is regarded as the official race meeting for the ordinary people.

Despite a perception, and at times its portrayal, as an integrated city, Galway is as socially segregated as any city in Ireland. Both east and west of the city contains working class areas with high unemployment and low spending power. Most of them are on the periphery of the city created to cater for families moved from their familiar inner city location and existing community networks. Low car ownership and poor quality public transport has resulted in social isolation as well as geographical segregation with consequential high levels of environmental vandalism and social dysfunction. These disadvantaged areas in Galway are both at the physical edge and margins of the city and at the symbolic edge and margins of Galway society.

Galway social and cultural life is not immune from its spectrum of contradictions. It is perceived as cosmopolitan and outgoing, yet is still quite small and at times very provincial and suffocating. Regarded as the cultural capital of Ireland, yet its cultural credentials are mainly confined to the performance area, and even then has a certain commercial awareness and edge to it. Noted for its traditional music, yet is often of the rowdy, pub music variety than the purist traditional type. Its portrayal as a place with a fun-loving, party atmosphere tends to conceal a strong culture of excessive teenage and student drinking. Often described as both colourful and vibrant, its typical weather condition is rain from grey leaden skies overhead. Its bohemian and left bank image contrasts with the crowded Galway Cathedral for the annual, nine-day solemn novena every February.

The best example, however, of Galway's flexible personality, its tussle with history and modernity, culture and commerce, Gaelic and English identity, was the decision in recent years to name all the fourteen road traffic roundabouts around the city after the Merchant Tribes of Galway and then proceed to display their names in Irish. With that act, the Tribes were unwittingly given a second Cromwellian rebuke for their vanity in proclaiming themselves Tribes, as in Roman Tribes, but as a friendly gesture were honoured and conferred for having become more Irish than the Irish themselves – confirmed in writing.

Part Three

Looking Ahead – What Kind of Future for Galway?

Introduction

Given the uncertain nature of Ireland's current economic situation, it might seem strange to start peering into the future to predict what's in store for Galway and, in particular, to map out a direction and vision for its continued growth and evolution. However, recessions are the ideal time to stop and take stock of where the city has come from and, crucially, where it needs to go from here. There is the qualified bonus that the city is unlikely to see significant activity in the city's growth in the short term, which allows the space and freedom to really consider its future expansion when it does occur. Already people are referring to this as possibly a lost decade. However, in this quiet period, if reflection brings a clear sense of purpose and direction, then in time it may be seen as a decade of gain.

This is the appropriate time to look at a fifty-year timeframe up to 2062, and even beyond to 2100, to consider both the city's short-term and long-term growth and change. In particular, it will focus the mind on the fact that Galway's population may increase by a similar figure of 50,000 in the next fifty years, as a conservative estimate, or may even double its population to 150,000 as an outside figure. Indeed, by the end of the century, Galway could be home to over 200,000, or three times its current population, based on its status as a designated Gateway City. This is in line with all prevailing trends and predictions, where 60 per cent of the Irish population now live in urban areas, which is set to further increase as we become a more urbanised society. These figures in many ways are frightening in the context of the size and population of the existing city, and that level of expansion will provide serious challenges requiring clear thinking to address them. However, Galway is not alone. Rapid urbanisation and the process of providing attractive homes, communities and cities are the challenges facing all urban areas, both nationally and internationally, irrespective of size.

The last fifty years have shown that Galway has not coped very well with unprecedented growth, but again it is not alone there. To look closely at the city centre and what was inherited fifty years ago, and then to study closely at what has been built around the periphery of that core, it is hard to argue that the created city edge is as inviting and attractive as its centre. Why is that? There is no simple direct answer. Modern cities are extremely complex systems made up of a mesh of people, lifestyles, machines, buildings, politics and power. The planning of cities is equally complex, combining a diverse range of inputs including land use, transportation, natural and built heritage, enterprise and employment, community and culture, environment and infrastructure, population and demographics. It is subject to national and international, cultural and social trends, fashions, lifestyles, guidelines, conventions and policies. Despite the complexity, it is important that citizens make themselves aware of the choices available in providing for a desirable city for themselves and handing it over to the next generation with a sense of place to be proud of.

In doing so, it is important to realise that the city is first and foremost for its citizens, a place where they can invest resources, energy and emotion – a place where its residents can live life. However, in a globalised and competitive commercial world, it is necessary to be conscious that Galway is also competing for inward investment from highly mobile international companies who have many options, not only on the availability of a skilled workforce and tax incentives, but on the quality of life of their chosen city. In addition, tourism, which is also a very competitive area, will continue to be one of Galway's most important economic sectors so retaining its distinctive sense of place is essential in order to be successful.

One of the great advantages of Galway's relatively small size, and having a history of being the talisman of progress over the centuries, is that it is not necessary to re-invent the wheel. There are numerous examples, particularly in continental Europe, of cities comparable to Galway that have successfully expanded and in the process either maintained or enhanced the quality of their environment. Equally, there are other examples, including the capital city of Dublin, of unsuccessful models of expansion which Galway can also learn from. Critically, however, there are also very good historical examples of modern trends in urban living in Galway City itself, which allows the city to consider where it needs to go without looking outside or abroad for all the answers. It is important that Galway doesn't combine the advantages of being latecomers to emerging high quality urban trends with the disadvantages of being slow learners to these examples of good practice. The secret in learning from others and from the past is firstly to correctly analyse the city as it stands, including its particular unique circumstances, secondly to critically examine all current models of excellence, and finally to adapt these selected elements of best practice to the local conditions of Galway. The overall aim is to create a city of beauty with an enduring sense of place.

By the end of the century, it is estimated that 70 to 80 per cent of the world's population will be living in cities, so in the context of the future growth of Galway it is important to understand the predominant current trends in city expansion, which is defined as the sustainable city. How does the concept translate into the future growth of cities? In broad terms, it is the art of creating and shaping cities more like those that existed prior to the rise of the motorcar in the middle of the twentieth century – a city that is more compact and connected, supports a range of different uses, allowing people to live, work and enjoy themselves at close quarters within an attractive urban environment, which is well served with public transport and adaptable to change, a place where people of all ages and circumstances want to live. It is not necessary to look beyond our existing, general city centre areas that we admire and like so much as an appropriate example, where there are interconnected streets and squares instead of roads and roundabouts, houses, shops, and offices instead of one use only, where once there were a mix of all age, social and household classes, creating a neighbourly community close or accessible to all necessary amenities and facilities – a liveable, human, walkable city with a strong sense of place. This new trend is designed to address the current prevailing forms of development which consist of suburban areas of low density housing with segregated suburban shopping, industrial, office, leisure and retail areas, which are all car-dependent and lead to increased traffic, social, financial and environmental problems, including congestion, increased personal and infrastructural costs, social isolation, lack of services and facilities. The sustainable city requires a major change in emphasis, in particular higher densities to create a sense of community which can support shops, services and public transport. It involves exploring alternative means of transport including walking, cycling, bus, tram and train. It encourages new types and form of homes, to cater for all household categories integrated with shops, workplace, leisure and amenity areas. Underpinning it is a need for higher quality design standards, both in building and the spaces between buildings, to foster a community capable of catering for the full range of human needs.

In looking to the future for Galway, however, it is first important to study its growth in a national context.

IRELAND AND CITIES

Cities do not feature prominently in the consciousness of Irish people. Even though 60 per cent of Irish people now live in urban centres, which continues to grow, very little thought or discussion is given to their significance. Even in general public discourse, commentary on urban life is mostly absent. The main reference to city living is the twice daily rush hour traffic report and the occasional reference to the property market. In TV, drama or art, urban life at times forms the backdrop but only through its extreme portrayal, either dereliction and urban blight or city centre activities and corporate image. The suburban world where most Irish people now live, work, shop and recreate is rarely a central focus, perhaps because of its banality and mundanity. This is in contrast to much of the developed and developing world where the topic of growing population, environmental issues and urbanisation are seen as important issues to be

Aerial view of Galway City

addressed. Why this lack of interest in the growth and change of cities in Ireland? There are a number of possible reasons.

It is often stated that Ireland is a rural culture, rooted in a rural tradition, where urbanisation is an aberration and seen as part of our colonial history. However, that argument has little validity today. A century ago Ireland had 70 per cent of its population living a rural life; today it is only 40 per cent. The image of an Ireland of dispersed, rural settlement living is no longer accurate. Indeed, that feature of Ireland was relatively short-lived in our history. Up to the pre-Famine era, Irish rural settlement was typically of a grouped 'clachan type', particularly in the areas now most imaged as rural Ireland, which indicates that the Irish preference was for proximity and adjacency rather than dispersal and isolation. Whilst the post-Famine re-ordering of the Irish landscape changed that, it only had a shelf life of less than a century before more urban tendencies reasserted themselves. This view is reinforced by the experience of Irish emigrants to America in the aftermath of the Famine, where they were drawn to the urban centres of New York, Boston and Philadelphia rather than rural

America, which was more popular with other European emigrants. Similarly, the fate of Irish emigrants in 1950s England tended to centre on the dense urban areas of London such as Kilburn, Camden and Cricklewood. While the idea of urban life, particularly Dublin, was associated in some nationalist minds as the remnants of colonialism, this dissolved with the new-found prosperity in the last fifty years. Paradoxically, the experience of rural Ireland migrating to the capital city was a preference for the higher density, Victorian terraces of Ranelagh, Rathmines and Rathgar because of convenience to the city, the attraction of a city community and the grandeur and elegance of the architecture.

The Irish view of cities is also thought to be a product of a relatively low density population in comparison to other European countries. Ireland's population of 4.5 million has one of the lowest densities in Europe. When one considers that Ireland had a population of almost double that at 8.5 million in 1845, while England then had a population of 18.5 million compared to its current population of 54 million, Ireland today, without the impact of the Famine and subsequent periods of mass emigration, could conceivably have a population in the region of 25 million. This would have forced Ireland to face up to the issue of urbanisation early in the twentieth century, rather than early in the twenty-first as is now the case. Even though the last fifty years has seen the transition from a majority rural population to a majority urban one, in terms of urban history this is a relatively recent phenomenon and at a relatively early stage in an indigenous urban tradition.

The suburban pattern of city growth which has been the predominant settlement type in Ireland in the last fifty years was not, in hindsight, inevitable. It evolved out of a particular set of social, economic and cultural circumstances that existed in 1960s Ireland. What was inevitable in looking for a new housing typology to meet the needs of the gradual drift into Irish towns and cities was to look abroad for an appropriate model. This search went no further than to our closest English-speaking cultural influences – England and later America. Even today, while Ireland may be a monetary and regulatory colony of continental Europe, it remains a cultural and economic colony of England and the United States – an Anglo-American hybrid society. Consequently, Ireland first imported the quintessential English development of suburban housing in the 1960s and 1970s, aided by the close interrelationship between English and Irish national house building companies and a deference to England's great history and tradition in urban living. Ironically, therefore, Ireland borrowed the new typology of suburbia, which was developed in England as a consequence of the Industrial Revolution – a revolution Ireland never had. Later the American influence became more overt in the form of suburban retailing and other centres of economic activity in the city periphery.

Translated to Ireland, suburban housing offered promise, the dream of affordable ownership, of an individual house (or at worst a semi-individual house) on its own site located in both the city and country, a sense of freedom, choice and individuality, all desires of the post-1960s generation. The simple device of separating closely adjoining houses into detached or semi-detached forms was seen to readily answer this desire, as well as providing a direct access to back gardens and even the economical cost-saving sharing of party walls and chimneys in semi-d's. Ultimately, this left the dreamer feeling shortchanged, as the repetitive pattern destroyed the independence they craved, the separation was a visual illusion and there was quickly a realisation that suburbia was neither the city nor the country. In hindsight, and now with regret, if the English model of suburbia had continued their own higher density, urban streetscape tradition, it would have been just as easily adapted to Irish suburbia, providing a greater sense of community, honest democracy and a more reassuring sense of enclosure.

One peculiar aspect of Ireland's relationship with suburbia, in a country and at a time where economics is dictating the agenda, is that people rarely see the connection between cities and the cost of living. Irish people tend to look at personal costs and budgets in a very immediate and direct way. Thus, house and household costs such as food, electricity, oil, gas, telephone and insurance are all obvious costs to be budgeted and paid as required, similar to state income tax and other similar taxes. However, cities impose a form of selective and indirect stealth tax which householders rarely scrutinize, because they are hidden and often lost in the mix of suburban living. These costs relate to transport costs, which for the average suburban resident can be either the first or second biggest weekly household cost that has to be met. Thus the recent controversial, annual household charge represents only an average weekly cost in fuelling the typical two-car suburban family. When car costs, depreciation, maintenance, tax and insurance are taken into account, transport costs arising from low density suburban living represent a multiple of the fixed household service costs. Consequently, people who live on public transport routes in cities, which are generally state-subsidised, and even people who live and work in small Irish towns and villages, enjoy a huge economic advantage to those who live in car-dependent suburbs or commuter areas. Accordingly, cities place a selective, invisible tax burden on Irish householders without their apparent awareness.

Ireland's general lack of understanding of cities is more attributable to the fact that cities lie outside the more immediate and everyday realm of their personal life and home. Cities by their scale and nature are incomprehensible and removed, in comparison to more personal, intimate and tangible experiences. Ironically, this lack of understanding can make Irish people very adaptable to change and open to new urban ways of living. In this regard, the last twenty years has seen the first generation of Irish people growing accustomed to city centre apartment living, which both confirms the ability to adapt and perhaps an ability to mutate into the wider and denser suburbia. The sustainable city, which is not new, just a rediscovery of former ways of city living, can easily integrate into the Irish experience. In this age of austerity, its main selling point initially may be economic, in the same way that CO_2 emissions linked to tax bands changed car buying behaviour and the energy rating of homes have impacted on customer preferences on home purchase. However, the discovery of community, sense of place and liveability can help seal its attraction and become the model for the growth and future of Irish city settlement patterns.

IRISH CITY PLANNING AND DEVELOPMENT

The growth and development of Irish cities is planned and controlled by individual city development plans. The requirement and process for providing these plans is set out in the 1963 Planning and Development Act and subsequent amendments, in particular the 2000 act. All city councils are instructed by law to make a development plan every six years, which becomes the blueprint for the physical, economic and social development of the city over its six-year lifespan. The process is demo-cratic and open with any interested individuals, groups or organisations at local, regional or national level allowed to make submissions for con-sideration by elected members of the council before the development plan is decided upon. The plan is normally drafted by the city council executive in consultation with the elected members. The overall aim of the development plan is to meet the objective future needs of the city in the interest of the common good, and consequently provides both the policy and framework for all subsequent local planning decisions. The Department of Environment, Heritage and Local Government, the Gov-ernment body with responsibilities in this area, issues guidelines from time to time, most notably in 2007, with their publication *Development Plans – Guidelines for Local Authorities*, which outlines the standards to achieve best practice in the making of development plans and taking into account all relevant national and regional guidelines.

One of the strengths of the document is that all city development plans are now reasonably consistent, but their uniformity and adoption of standard text is also a weakness as it can lead to a lack of real thought and analysis at local level. This can result in a bland, jargoned and lazy document that is useful as a box ticking exercise for assessing individual planning applications but offers no particular vision for different and distinctive cities. However, the problems with modern city development plans are more deep-rooted than that, and it is questionable whether they are now fit for purpose in their current format. Indeed, looking back, it is doubtful whether they were ever fit for purpose, although it is easy to be wise in hindsight. However, the evolution of Irish cities since the in-troduction of the Planning Acts in 1963 would tend to support that view.

The first major problem with city development plans is their restric-tion to six-year timelines. The forward planning of cities over six years is simply insufficient to develop medium and long-term strategies for their change and growth. The current problems with Irish cities have occurred because of incremental changes over multiple six-year periods that were never predicted or planned for. Having to take a longer-term view over fifty years, as well as a short term of six years, would focus attention on dealing with a doubling or trebling of the population and requiring a more radical appraisal of the primary twin elements of settlement and transport. A fifty-year long-term plan for Irish cities back in the early 1960s would arguably have yielded very different cities today. Obviously, any fifty-year period would still have to be reviewed every six years in light of changing demographics and trends, but it is the only logical way to deal with high population increases, which over a short period have less impact and are more incidental. Crucially, the constantly evolving fifty-year parent plan would inform and provide the strategies for the six-year fixed interim plan.

The second drawback with current development plans is their formulation by narrowly focussed disciplines and mindsets. The general responsibility for providing city plans within the city council executive lies with professional planners in cooperation with the various engineering departments. These disciplines are insufficiently broad in scope, skills and knowledge to deal with the complex issues of city building. To create a comprehensive city plan that is rooted in a local identity requires the additional discipline of urban design and urban economics. Urban design would bring a wider vision of the city to the plan and the necessary skills to implement that vision. Urban design is often used after the development plan stage in the form of local area plans. However this is often too late as LAPs, notwithstanding their quality, are often misplaced if the base development plan is flawed. While urban economics may seem a strange bedfellow with urban design, the future vision for any city must be underpinned and reinforced by economic realities and viable investment. The fusion of all four disciplines is necessary to produce city development plans that are creative and able to achieve attractive, liveable cities.

The third major fault with current city development plans is in their approach and presentation. All development plans use two dimensional maps, both during the process and afterwards in its final adopted version. This method has been used since its inception fifty years ago with the only visible change in that time being the fairly unremarkable move from black and white to colour maps in the last ten to fifteen years. A two

3D modelling of medieval Galway as a reference

dimensional mindset to address the needs of humans and cities, both of which exist in three dimensions, is too crude an approach to city evolution, and provides only a surface, quantitative rather than a deeper qualitative analysis. Living in a high tech age, where communication devices are becoming increasingly sophisticated, with the advent of 3D city modelling, the availability of Google Earth and Google Map Street View, it is unnecessary to be relying on an outdated format that neither optimises the planning and design of cities nor is customer friendly.

Current city development plans are mostly written in a language destined to alienate citizens of the city they are purporting to represent. The idea that city development documents could be produced, presented and marketed in a way that local city book shops and citizens could be enticed to purchase them has never been explored, mainly because they are produced in expert rather than everyday language. In general, the language of development plans needs to be more accessible, relevant and consumer friendly. The city development plan should simply become the city plan; new zoned development areas should simply become growth areas with no fixed zoning; existing zoned areas should become areas with no fixed zoning; office and industrial use should be stated as work areas; residential use should be changed to home areas; retail as shop areas; educational as learning areas and so on. In that way city plans start to become more humanised, and in a language that citizens could start to identify with, leading to a greater appreciation, interest and understanding of their city.

There are other issues with current city development plans which also need to be addressed. Since the introduction of the concept of creating sustainable cities over ten years ago, the most extraordinary and incredible omission in all recent city plans is the simple statistic of the city's existing density, which is the first and key indicator of a city's status, position and ability to achieve sustainability, particularly in terms of land use, settlement and transport. It remains the most revealing piece of data on the general form, compactness and nature of the city.

All plans should include short, medium and long-term achievable targets, which should be specifically reviewed in subsequent plans to determine and comment on their achievement or progress. Given the pattern of development in the last fifty years targets for increasing density is an obvious example. Plans need to be more conscious of their specific location. They need to describe the essence of the city physically, culturally and socially, and identify the elements that make it unique and how that distinctiveness can be a template for expansion. Crucially, it needs to provide clarity on where the city is at, where it needs to go and what needs to be done to get there. City plans need to put the shorter six-year plans in a broader, national and international context, in particular in terms of economic activity. None of the current development plans gives a clear sense that Ireland and Europe are experiencing economic turmoil, which directly impacts on city change and growth. City plans should specifically identify and name existing structural problems within the city, based on all current thinking and prevailing trends, and devise means to address these issues. Finally, there is a sense that development plans are preoccupied with strategies, policies, objectives and processes rather than the fundamental aims of creating beautiful cities which people are proud of and enjoy living in. There is a sense that development plans do not cater for the unconventional, the unexpected and the surprising, all vital elements of historic cities that both citizens and visitors are attracted and drawn to.

SUSTAINABILITY

The concept of sustainability, which is largely defined as meeting the needs of the present without compromising future development, was officially adopted into Irish law with the passing of the 2000 Planning and Development Act. This act supports the idea that all future development be sustainable in economic, social and environmental terms. While the term itself is overused, abused and at this stage colonised by most sectors of Irish society, it has a critical role in the growth of urban areas. Two elements are key to achieving sustainability in Irish cities: transport and density. Transport is the largest single element in Irish energy use and in order to meet our international commitment, the Department of Transport is aiming for a 60/40 per cent split between sustainable means of transport versus the motor car by 2020. Given the state's vast investment in roads as opposed to rail and bus since 2000, it is hard to understand how that objective can be met.

The current interest in sustainable transport is now also driven by the recent spike in fuel prices and an acknowledgment that the passing of the oil age is imminent. Sustainable transport is now defined as transport which aids the mobility of one generation without compromising the mobility of future generations, with the key being the implementation of a transport hierarchy which gives priority to the pedestrian and public systems over the car. The exploration of alternative means of transport has focussed on the different transport modes which were popular prior to the rise in use of the motor car in the twentieth century, including walking, which was the first and still most sustainable form, the bus, dating back to the seventeenth century, the tram, rail and cycling which were developed in the nineteenth century.

However, central to the policy of sustainable transport is the settlement patterns of our cities and it is now accepted that increased densities in our cities are vital to support viable alternative means of transport. The internationally accepted criterion of minimum, sustainable, gross population density is sixty persons per hectare. This criterion is based on both the spatial, qualitative and economic requirements to create compact cities that can support and optimise community participation, public transport, commercial services, civic and social services, public infrastructural networks and a general complexity and diversity of functions and people. The increased densities have been incorporated into city development plans in the last ten years, but with the slowdown in the economy since 2007, it is difficult to gauge its impact to date. In addition, both the optional and mandatory requirements for more detailed local area plans within city development plan areas are also incorporated. However, these initiatives to improve densities tend to be used for new rather than existing developments and highlight a major flaw in the pursuit of sustainable cities.

The vast majority of development in Irish cities in the last fifty years has occurred in low density suburban areas, between a third and a half of the new recommended densities. Most of older suburbia is now experiencing an ageing and declining population, as families grow and move out. With Irish average household sizes now closer to the European norm at 2.6 persons, these older suburban homes with three and four bedrooms have even a lower average. This has resulted in vast suburban areas of our cities of low density, compounded by lower average occupancy, with larger than average required homes of today. The idea of having a dense urban centre and new high density developments on the periphery, while maintaining the underused, low density middle, equates to a bicycle wheel with a dense hub, an inflated tyre on its rim, connected with spokes but little density. This is the antithesis of the traditional city, where density follows a progressive and gradual pattern out from the core, which is vital to sustain alternative means of transport. In es-

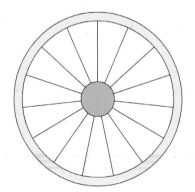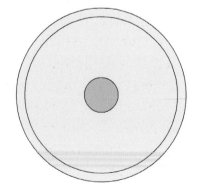

Spoked wheel city growth vs disk wheel city growth

sence, what is required is 'refurbia', or suburban renewal, similar to urban renewal of the 1980s, which alters and increases the density of existing suburban areas and changes the traditional spoked bicycle wheel to the new, solid disc wheel, which will help address and in time reconcile the sprawling nature of our existing cities.

Making this happen requires radical thinking including restricting the zoning of all new housing developments to within the outer perimeter edges of the city, a review of current standards in regard to overlooking and car parking, and the mandatory requirement to upgrade all existing altered houses to current energy standards in the process of increasing its density. With that approach, two crucial components of sustainability are being addressed – existing houses are upgraded to reduce emissions and sustainable transport is made more viable. The argument that existing suburbia be allowed to age and waste naturally for future replacement is contrary to the idea of sustainability, where existing houses contain a significant element of embodied energy which is lost when replaced. This targeted approach to altering and increasing the density of existing suburbia will not get universal support, particularly from the construction and even design professions, where greenfield development is more straight forward and less troublesome. Indeed, for some local residents it is also likely to lead to resistance and objection. However, undoing the mistakes and wastage of the last fifty years requires drastic and radical surgery and will not be painless. The rewards in terms of sustainability are obvious and it remains the most logical and rational approach to intensify our cities in a more sustainable, holistic and sequential way.

The advantages do not end there, however. Suburban renewal would help to revitalise aging communities bringing a new age mix and energy. It would allow the now grown children of the neighbourhood the option of returning to their original community and their family network, providing the continuity that helps create permanent and stable communities. It would halt the decline in existing suburban schools, both primary and secondary, and reduce the necessity to build new ones. It would stabilise and reinforce the use of existing community, social, health and commercial services built up over the years, reducing the demand to create new ones. It would optimise the use of existing infrastructural services such as roads, sewers, drains, electricity, communications and gas, and help to reduce the expansion of such services. Finally, it would elevate existing suburbs to the density they should always have been, to avoid the wasteful resource of land and sufficiently dense to support viable public transport. If one accepts the logic and need for increased density, this logic also suggests that the higher densities should be from the city core out and not from the periphery out.

Linked to this initiative, Irish cities also need to tackle the issue of segregated zoning of land use if it is serious about achieving the ideal of sustainability. The continuance of the outdated notion of separating use, which has been prevalent for the last fifty years, has been identified as one of the key obstacles to creating sustainable cities. Unfortunately, it is also one of the most difficult issues to address as it is now so firmly embedded in city life and continues to form the main plank of the urban planning of our cities. The process should start with the simple acknowledgement that zonings such as 'industrial' are no longer relevant, as society has moved on and that use has morphed into an office-based, clean process which has little relevance to the former traditional understanding of the word. From that, it is easier to imagine the idea of home, work, shop and recreation coalescing and creating genuinely compact and mixed use environments that were a traditional feature of our historic cities.

GALWAY'S PARTICULAR CHARACTERISTICS

In exploring a future vision for Galway City, it is worthwhile to quickly review the critical elements in its growth to date as covered in Part I of this book. This will help to summarise the historical context for its expansion for the remainder of this century and define its current base from which it will further develop.

Galway was founded and grew steadily within a relatively small walled enclosure of 13 hectares on the eastern shore of the River Corrib estuary, where it enters Galway Bay, from the thirteenth to the seventeenth century, after which it experienced long periods of stagnation. Despite never experiencing the great city development of the Georgian period as in Dublin, Limerick or Cork, Galway started to expand beyond its city walls to the east and west during the eighteenth century, but still re-

	Medieval city		1962
	1862		2012

mained very compact. In the first half of the nineteenth century, the city further evolved into the general form we experience today in its city centre in terms of public streets, spaces, buildings and infrastructure. The first accurate mapping of the city in 1838 still indicates a relatively dense city centred on the original medieval walled town. The post-Famine century from 1860 to 1960 was one of sharp decline and very slow recovery, where by 1971 the population had only recovered to its 1821 level. That century was marked by an expansion of its working class housing stock, the construction of two hospitals to both the east and west of the city, the continued drift of the middle class to its approach roads and the development of Salthill as a separate village holiday resort.

The half century period from the early 1960s to today has seen the greatest expansion and change in the city in terms of its population and footprint. During that era the city more than trebled its population and expanded its built environment over ten-fold into its rural hinterland

and changed from being a relatively compact and dense city to a more dispersed and loose one. The city also changed from a mono-centred city, with a satellite centre of Salthill, to a multi-centred city, as it developed a series of centres of activity around its suburban peripheral areas. During that last fifty years, Galway also consolidated its status as the regional capital on the western seaboard by expanding its industrial base, developing its educational facilities, nurturing its cultural life and increasing its tourism business. Today, the city is both portrayed and branded at different times as a maritime city, a city of learning, a city of culture and in recent times as a centre for healthcare and IT development. However, its perception as a tourist city is now its most enduring image.

The accompanying map highlights the evolution of the city from its birth to today in terms of its footprint area, population and density. It demonstrates that Galway rapidly lost its compactness as a city in just the last fifty years of its 750 year evolution, to the point where today it falls well short of the density, internationally recognised, as required to be a sustainable city. Consequently, Galway needs to double its current density from thirty to sixty persons per hectare, which is halfway to the density of ninety which it enjoyed in the early 1960s. Despite the city having a very positive image based on its social, cultural and tourist ambiance, the natural and built heritage of the medieval city centre and vast stock of water attractions, behind the mask is the hidden city of its suburban sprawling edge, where most of its citizens now live, work, shop and recreate, and through which visitors move through as quickly as traffic allows to get to the main attraction at its core.

This is the context in which Galway's continued evolution should be explored. This needs to be done within the wider context of the national consensus for the future growth of cities already outlined. It also needs to be done in the context of the recent unsustainable past of the city and country, a more frugal and economically challenging future which ironically can encourage rather than impede a better quality prospect. A large part of that process is about reclaiming some of the qualities that make the historical city so attractive, and which were lost in the last fifty years.

This will require a certain independence of thought and action, due to the discrepancy between the rhetoric and reality of national policy, and at times challenge the basis of some current state attitudes. Crucially, it will also require challenging the now embedded attitudes of the city as a result of two generations of lost direction and purpose. This independent stance and vision may require invoking the spirit of the original 'Tribes of the City' who went outside the state and particularly to continental Europe to create an independent city with a physical quality that continues to endure and be enjoyed today.

Identifying the unique characteristics of the city that are relevant to its future growth is essential in order to critically analyse where Galway is positioned at this junction in its history. Some have already been highlighted in previous sections, while others are less obvious but equally important in providing a reference to its future growth. Below are a few of the most relevant characteristics not previously outlined.

Geography, Access and Entrance

While Galway shares with Dublin and Cork a similar semi-circular city boundary outline centred on its main river axis as it enters the sea, it differs from both cities, and deviates completely from Limerick, in terms of its geography and primary access into the city. Galway City occupies a relatively narrow neck of land only 4 kilometres wide between two vast impermeable expanses of water – Lough Corrib to the north and Galway Bay/Lough Atalia to the south. This is one of the reasons why Galway has historically expanded to both east and west of the river and less to the north. Access from the city is from east, west and north, each side of Lough Corrib. However, because of its distinctive neckline and location between the more populated east and less populated west, the majority of commuter movement and practically all of the visitor movement into the city is from the east. Consequently, the vast majority of traffic accessing the city is from the east and north east of the city.

In comparison to Dublin and Cork, which have a semi-circle, and Limerick which has a full circle, approach area for traffic into their cities, Galway's primary traffic approach occupies just a confined quadrant area to the east of the city. This is why the daily traffic report on Galway

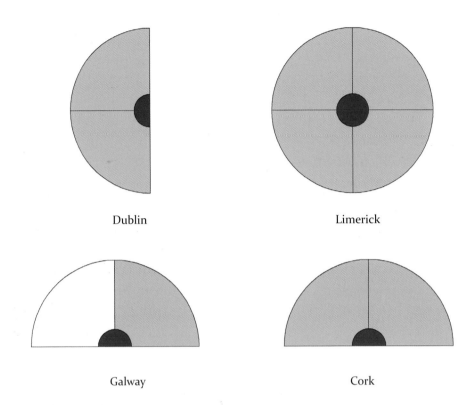

Dublin

Limerick

Galway

Cork

Main traffic approaches to city centres in Ireland

generally refers to only the Dublin, Tuam and Headford approach roads in terms of traffic congestion, which tends to further intensify during the summer season. This is compounded by all of the industrial and sub-urban office areas of the city, located to the east, with the west almost exclusively residential, creating a highly concentrated focus on the east city for both commuters and city based workers. This geography and access quadrant is the primary reason that the city is more prone to traffic congestion in proportion to its population compared to the other main cities in Ireland.

The main combined commuter and visitor entrance to the city was the Dublin Road, now changed and repositioned to the M6 motorway approach road. This recent change has completely altered both the sense and tone of its main entry point. Previously the Dublin Road access provided a very soft, positive and gradually revealing entrance by Merlin Park woods and GMIT, with occasional glimpses of the sea, before the

*Original main entrance to the city from the east by Merlin Park Woods (top)
and new main entrance from the east by Ballybrit (bottom)*

final attractive view of Lough Atalia prior to the arrival at the city centre. The new entrance now cuts through the typical suburban edge developments of shopping centres, retail parks, warehousing, fast food outlets, car showrooms, industrial estates and a plethora of signage, creating a totally different, generally negative experience which is lacking in local identity and a sense of the city of Galway.

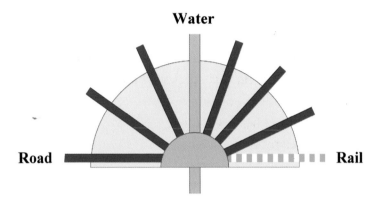

Conduits into the city

Topography and Conduits of the City

Galway is generally regarded as a relatively flat city, however towards the east and west the terrain becomes more undulating and in parts hilly. In general, the topography of the city could be described as gentle, undulating slopes, with occasional hillier terrain each side of the flat River Corrib plain. The city's landform, therefore, while more severe than Dublin or Limerick but less than Cork, provides no obstacle to walking or cycling as a practical means of transport.

The primary conduits into and through the city is its road network, which tends to be primarily on an east/west axis with four bridge crossings of the river. There are four main approach roads from the east, Dublin Road, Tuam Road, Headford Road and Monivea Road, which divide into three routes into the city centre and one inner bypass. From the west there are two main approach roads, the Barna Road and Moycullen Road, which separate into two main routes into the city centre and one inner bypass. The second conduit into the city is the rail line, which enters and terminates at the city centre from the east, flanking the eastern shoreline of the bay. The third conduit into the city is water, both saltwater and freshwater. The sea harbour provides a highway into the heart of the city for shipping and sailing craft. The lake harbour at Woodquay terminates the corridor into the city core from Lough Corrib to the north via the River Corrib. The accompanying diagram illustrates the principle conduits of the city.

Water Frontage, Open Space and Village Centres

Galway's natural heritage provides the city with a unique variety of water bodies and watercourses. Its vast stock of water provides the city with an incredible 65 kilometres of water frontage, most of which has yet to be exploited for its amenity and scenic value. This water frontage includes the obvious shoreline of Galway Bay from Rusheen Bay to Oranmore Bay, the banks of the River Corrib and Eglinton Canal, around Lough Atalia and the southern shore of Lough Corrib. One of the notable changes in the characteristics of the city in the last fifty years is in the city's relationship with water. The historic city, including its traditional resort village of Salthill, has a very direct and immediate relationship to water, with the built heritage creating a strong and enclosing edge to the natural heritage of its water bodies and watercourses. This is most evident on the banks of the River

*Open space to River Corrib,
1 kilometre from Eyre Square*

Corrib and canal at the city centre and the sea frontage of Salthill. In the modern era this tendency has changed to one of retreat from water to maintain a separating zone for expanded amenity use, which alters the nature of the relationship to a more open, weaker and less urban one.

In the modern era, the characteristics of the city's open space has developed considerably. Now there is a diverse sequence and hierarchy of public open spaces which vary from the traditional spaces like Eyre Square to the new passive spaces of sea and riverfronts, from the semi-public spaces of housing areas to public recreational parks, and from large sports and leisure open spaces to small incidental public areas. The quantity of open space in the city has increased incrementally and in sequence with the growth of the city. However, the quality and nature of some of the open space provision is questionable, and in a location where there is insufficient population to use, support and enjoy it.

Another characteristic of the city is the idea of a village centre which is separate from the main city, of which Salthill was the only example in the developed historic city. Both centres grew very slowly and separately during the nineteenth and twentieth centuries and only came together to form part of the now expanded city in the modern period. The concept of a smaller village centre and community within a large city is quite common in Ireland, particularly in Dublin, and has a similar focus of city activity that rural towns and villages provide in rural Ireland. Consequently, Salthill is a useful model of that type of city sub-centre, which can provide for a more localised identity within a larger and expanding city. However, it is noticeable that in the last fifty years of Galway's expansion, and despite its population increasing over three-fold and its footprint over ten-fold, no other village sub-centre has been created which would have broken down the amorphous suburbs and provided a better sense of community, belonging and place.

Urban Mindset

The final characteristic of the city is a subconscious, psychological trait rather than a visible physical one – that of an urban mindset, or to be more accurate, the lack of an urban mindset. While Galway is referred to as a city and technically has all the ingredients of population, services, facilities and amenities of one, it has more of a sense of a town, or to be more precise, an overgrown town. That sense has a number of contributing components. The relatively small, compact nature of its city centre of medieval origin is still relatively intact despite the recent high growth

Rural scene in the city, 1.5 kilometres from Eyre Square

of its periphery. The lack of a Georgian imprint in the eighteenth and nineteenth centuries deprived the city of a more urban scale and feel, particularly beyond its immediate city centre. The relatively abrupt transition from the city centre scale to the suburban scale is quite obvious in Galway, particularly to the east of the city where within walking distance of Eyre Square the city becomes noticeably suburban relatively quickly. Finally, the huge suburban expansion of the city has bestowed it with a much larger proportional element of low density settlement relative to the small, higher density core. These features of the city have resulted in it lacking the scale, drama and urban feel of even its nearest and comparable sized city of Limerick, despite its obvious attraction as a city. Consequently, there is a sense of Galway lacking an urban mindset, despite its size and population. That characteristic is very important in the context of creating a more sustainable city, which will require it to become more dense, higher in scale and more urban in feel. The challenge in making that transition is to subtly adopt a new urban mindset without compromising its sense of place.

Galway's Future Growth

Galway's short-term future evolvement is planned and controlled by the City Development Plan, as devised by Galway City Council, which is reviewed every six years. The current plan from 2011 to 2017 generally conforms to guidelines as set down by the parent state agency, the Department of the Environment, Local Government and Heritage, which has an overseeing responsibility in this area. Consequently, the present plan contains all the shortcomings and inadequacies of all city plans as highlighted in the previous section, 'Irish City Planning and Development'. This includes an insufficient timeframe for forward planning, lack of a broader and more holistic involvement, a two rather than a three

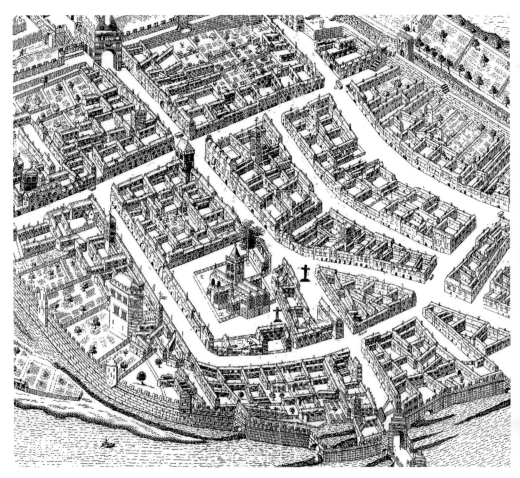

Pictorial Map 1651

172

dimensional approach, an alienating language and presentation, and the absence of indentifying urban problems and issues that need to be addressed on an ongoing basis. In reviewing the existing city plan, it is necessary to see the impact of these shortcomings in the local context of Galway. More importantly, however, it is revealing to examine and analyse the particular proposals for the future of the city as set down in the plan.

As a starting point, it is interesting to compare the 1651 pictorial map of Galway City with the corresponding 2011 city plan map of the city. The 1651 map is a three dimensional depiction of the city, part real, part imagined. However, despite its embellishments, it seeks to portray a very developed vision and image for the city in the seventeenth century – it is imagining the city as it could be at some future date. The 2011 part

Development Map 2011

map is a twenty-first century, two dimensional version of the city that has neither a vision nor an imagined future. In many ways it is hard to comprehend or explain that the two dimensional approach is contemporary and supersedes the three dimensional vision by 360 years – a case of a 360 year advance, but a 360 degree reversal.

The general policy of the Galway City Development Plan is to 'facilitate the future strategies and sustainable development of Galway City as a Gateway City having regard to the recommendation of the Galway Transportation and Planning Study'. Galway is projected to increase its population in the short term to 100,000 by 2025, and to meet that need, the main direction for new settlement for the city is to be the Ardaun area, a bank of land to the east of the city towards the town of Oranmore, most of which ironically is in the County Council area, which confirms the inefficiency and ineffectiveness of having two separate bodies with responsibility for a relatively small city. This proposed expansion of the city in the one area was identified and recommended in the Galway Transportation and Planning Study, an independent study carried out in 1999, so it is first necessary to review that study. The study area comprised an area within a 30 mile radius of Galway City and adopted 1996 as the base year and 2011 as the design year.

In reviewing the study, it is only necessary to focus on the areas that solely apply to the city. The key lies not in the answers given, but in the questions asked of the study. The study proceeds on the basis of expanding the city rather than looking at the city as it currently exists and exploring opportunities for growth. Consequently, no analysis was carried out on the city's existing status, including its form and density, and how it compares with other cities in terms of sustainability and transportation. Therefore, the basis for the study was flawed from the start due to an inadequate and narrow brief. The fact that the study was carried out prior to the concept of sustainability becoming enshrined in Irish law in 2000 may be a factor. However, as it later transpires, the introduction of sustainability has not altered mindsets. The study proceeded to consider four different possible locations for the expansion of the city around its peripheral edge ranging from the Barna corridor to the west to the Ardaun corridor to the east (see accompanying map). These areas were

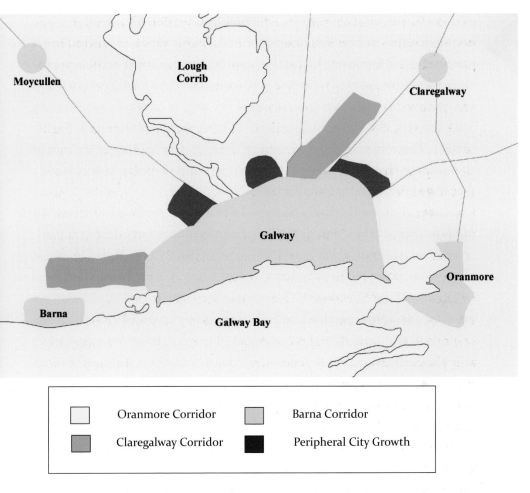

Moycullen

Lough
Corrib

Claregalway

Galway

Oranmore

Barna

Galway Bay

☐ Oranmore Corridor ▦ Barna Corridor

▦ Claregalway Corridor ■ Peripheral City Growth

evaluated and scored under a set of criteria based on transportation, public utilities, community facilities, impact on existing development and socioeconomic factors, with Ardaun emerging as the preferred option. Notwithstanding that, all selection processes are based on objective criteria that ultimately are subject to subjective assessment, and that the brief itself was initially lacking, the evaluation criteria in this case was too narrow and limited.

The study was a standard, planning and engineering analysis based on hard data and facts, but which ignored the soft data of how cities are experienced and observed. Unless a broader, holistic approach is taken when studying how Galway needs to evolve, it will continue to grow with the same lack of desirability and attraction as the last fifty years. The Planning and Transportation Study should have included a range of other criteria, mostly of soft values, which ironically are the values that guide our preference in how we experience and enjoy cities and where we are prepared to invest energy, emotion and resources. These additional criteria would include such diverse components as the form and structure of the city, the character and nature of the city, connection and identity with the city, the spirit and memory of the city, sequential and organic growth, the image and perception of the city, the natural environment of landform and landcover, potential variety and diversity, the liveability factor and the sustainability factor.

These additional criteria may not have altered the final outcome, but by introducing other ingredients into the mix it does force a fresh and different look at how Galway might grow. The natural extension of the logic that supports the 1999 study, based on the same criteria, is the continued expansion of the city towards Oranmore, until they eventually merge and become one, large, narrow band of an urban metropolis, straddling the motorway and dual carriageway access to the city from the east. If this is what emerges as being necessary, then it requires a significant long-term vision of how this is managed, envisioned and built. However, it is not clear or self-evident that is the case. The proposed Ardaun expansion of the city is a new and unprecedented departure from the historic progressive evolution of the city, and in its logical conclusion to merge with Oranmore would bestow on Galway a one-sided, linear, city form, unknown anywhere in Ireland. In reality, Ardaun will be a satellite area of the city's suburbs, over six kilometres from Eyre Square and cut off by its enclosing road network of dual carriageway, motorway and busy airport road. The area will have more of a physical, social and commercial connection to Oranmore than the city, leading to further erosion of its function as the city's commercial centre. Given its remove and surrounding road network, cycling and walking beyond its boundaries will not be possible, and if the only 13 per cent projected increase in public transport use – of a system that does not even exist at present – is realised, then Ardaun, with a potential population of over 18,000, will be a car-dependent community adding to Galway's eastside traffic congestion.

Simply put, there is no logic in further expanding and extending an already low density, dispersed city without first looking to intensify the

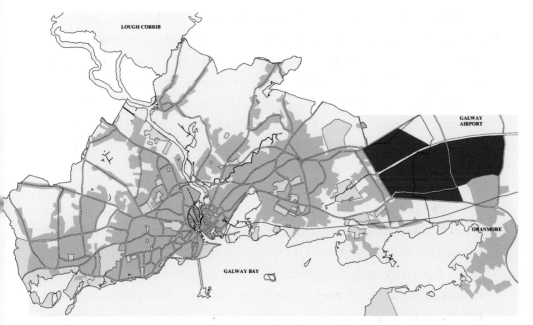

Planned expansion of city to merge with Oranmore for a population of 18,000

existing city. However, the city plan not only fails to encourage consolidation, it actively discourages it with a series of policies which are in direct contradiction to its own stated strategies and that of national policy for a sustainable city. These policies are centred on the existing suburbs of Galway and what is not permitted. Thus, no redevelopment of the outer suburbs is allowed and no demolition of existing dwellings for higher density replacement dwellings or apartments is acceptable in the inner or established suburbs. So, while most city development plans in the country at least allow the prospect of increasing densities in existing suburbs to the new recommended levels, the Galway City plan actively prevents it, which is in conflict with the whole concept of a compact and sustainable city, as enshrined in national law since 2000.

In addition, the city plan only applies the lower end of higher densities for new residential projects as recommended back in 1999. In the last ten years in Galway, new suburban residential provision has seen an equal mixture of apartments and traditional housing designed to a maximum density of 0.46. This has yielded just fourteen houses per acre (thirty-five per hectare), well below the maximum recommendation of twenty per acre (fifty per hectare) and significantly below the international norm for sustainable cities of twenty-four per acre (sixty per hectare) gross minimum. This lower scale of density for new housing combined with the existing low density of six to eight per acre (fifteen to twenty per hectare) is merely adding to Galway's difficulty in creating a concentrated city and the challenge of providing a high use, public transport system.

In the city centre a density of 2.0 still applies and has done for most of the last fifty years. However, as the city increase its population to 100,000 and beyond, it is no longer sustainable or economical to maintain that historical density in the three identified expansion areas for the city centre in the future, namely Ceannt Station, the Harbour Area and Inner Headford Road. A minimum density of 3.0 is now necessary in any expansion to the city centre, particularly in light of its proximity to the main transport hub of Ceannt Station and the future discouragement and requirement for car access and car parking in future city centre developments in preference to public transport. In the suburbs, the concept of still maintaining some low density housing areas, because of an existing pattern, is also no longer tenable, in light of sustainable land use. If the existing pattern militates against the higher density, the lands should simply remain unzoned. However, it is possible to provide high density adjacent to low density if sufficient separation or other devices are employed in order to create the preferable, high density as the new established pattern of development.

In summary, the current Galway City plan shows little sense of change of emphasis or direction since the introduction of the concept of sustainable cities in 2000, despite all the stated intentions contained in its policies. The city continues to remain in the grip of a suburban rather than urban mindset, which will frustrate any desire to build a compact city in the future that can viably support and encourage a sustainable transport system.

Traffic and Transport

As with all other major cities in Ireland, the primary discussion in the city of Galway, with all its physical, social, economic and cultural challenges, is on its perceived traffic problems. This perception has resulted in continuous local media attention and commentary, reinforced by the national media's twice daily traffic report on the city, special sittings of the city council to try to address the issue, local initiatives to garner public opinion, hotly divided opinions on the merits of roundabout versus traffic junctions to ease the problem, and a general acceptance and perhaps weary resignation that Galway has, and will continue to have, traffic problems. The irony of course is that Galway does not have a traffic problem – it has a transport problem. Galway is no different from any other national or even international city, where in the absence of a transport system traffic will continue to increase to a point of what's known as 'tolerable congestion'. Again, as in the issue of creating a sustainable city, Galway does not need to re-invent the wheel, but just inform itself on how the problem has been dealt with successfully in other similar cities and adopt the solution to suit local conditions.

The first principle arising out of the lesson of traffic research is that more, or wider, roads, revised junctions or any refinement of the traffic network will not solve the problem. It has been shown that cars will always simply increase to fill any new capacity back to the point of 'toler-

Proposed Outer City Bypass

179

able congestion'. Of course Galway has already experienced this feature with the opening of the new Quincentennial Bridge and four lane roadway in the mid-1980s, which was predicted to solve the city's traffic problems but which within ten years had reverted to the previous congestion. Proving that amnesia has a generational timespan, the same predictions are now being made for the new proposed city bypass. Although it is impossible to accurately predict public behaviour, the likelihood is that the bypass will have even less of a traffic impact than the Quincentennial Bridge because of its more singular function of catering for traffic between Connemara and the east of the city.

The second principle is that the development of an alternative transport system is the one and only method whereby traffic congestion has been successfully addressed in any city in the world. Despite all the experimentation with traffic signalling, one way streets and road widening, no city in the world has addressed traffic congestion without introducing a sustainable transport system.

The final principle is that there is no quick-fix solution to traffic congestion problems. The implementation of an alternative transport system is an on-going, long-term process, and the transition from car addiction to more sustainable uses is a slow and on-going cultural shift that requires a varied mixture of education, encouragement, restriction and sanction – a typical carrot and stick approach. The key to that shift is understanding that cars do not cause congestion – people do. Consequently, addressing it requires changing people's attitudes, habits and behaviour in terms of their car use and dependency.

The first critical awareness required to alter public behaviour is the understanding that Galway's commercial city core has a finite capacity to accommodate the private car because of its historical layout and street network. That capacity will always fill up quickly to create persistent city traffic congestion. However, while traffic congestion has considerable economic and environmental consequences, it does ironically have a crucial benefit in that it eventually forces changes in transport policy, which leads to change in car use. It is curious that in each city that has successfully addressed the problem the process goes through the same three stages of development, from the initial criticizing stage, through to the questioning phase, to the final acceptance stage. It would be ground-breaking if Galway could go straight to the final stage, on the basis of other city's experiences, but it seems every city needs to go through this torturous process before arriving at the same inevitable conclusion.

The option of doing nothing is neither advisable nor practical, and would be similar to removing the water control weir gates of the River Corrib which would immediately flood the city centre area. A number of years ago, during the Galway Races, the city became totally gridlocked which forced car users to abandon their cars on the roadways for a number of hours. A do nothing approach would lead to persistent examples of that scenario. Already Galway City is seen as a difficult city to access, particularly from the east. There is evidence that the fairly recent opening of the M6 motorway has ironically encouraged potential shoppers in East Galway and beyond to travel in the other direction, to Athlone and other towns, because of their perception of having less traffic and easier access. Consequently, Galway's traffic congestion has two major economic impacts – the actual and the perceived. The common misapprehension that gradually restricting car traffic in order to transfer existing road capacity to sustainable transport use will only have a negative effect on business is not accurate. The opposite is actually the case, where a sustainable transport system will greatly improve and enhance the commercial life of the city of which the pedestrianisation of Shop Street is an excellent example. Unfortunately, changing from car dependency to public transport is a long, difficult and often disruptive process, and is a classic Catch-22 situation. People will only make the switch if the sustainable system is attractive, reliable, frequent, economical and, most importantly, provides the journeys they wish to make. However, the provision of such a system requires sufficient numbers in order to make the necessary level of service viable. Having a good system is becoming increasingly important for cities. A recent survey of office-based companies in Dublin revealed that proximity to public transport was the single biggest factor in locating their headquarters.

During Christmas, the most concentrated period of traffic congestion in the city, Galway City Council operates a very low cost and successful

Park and Ride Scheme from Galway Racecourse to the city centre which caters for up to 2,000 passengers per day. It indicates a willingness on the part of the public to utilise sustainable transport if a regular, comfortable and cost effective option is provided. However, Galway City has only a 9 per cent public transport usage (4 per cent for work trips) because of a perception that the service is not reliable, frequent or extensive, and is well short of the target of 19 per cent by 2020 and 41 per cent for walking, cycling and other means, in order to meet the Department of Transport's overall target of 60 per cent for total alternative travel use. The main reason for this is because public transport was underfunded in the past, in comparison to the road network, which has left it with a very poor image. In addition, Galway's pattern of settlement and expansion in the last fifty years makes it very difficult and expensive to provide a viable and extensive service because of its low density and wide series of sub-centre areas of activity in the suburbs.

Paradoxically, however, the high investment in road infrastructure in the past can now assist in a sustainable transport system as the extra lanes provided in the city road network can be reallocated to dedicated bus or other alternative transport corridors, as has been successfully introduced in Dublin. This is where the first path of resistance is likely to be met, as previous car routes become exclusive mass transit routes, which tend initially to be very unpopular. However, as part of the education process the sight of alternative transport travelling past on a dedicated lane, while car users are stuck in traffic jams, is one of the painful lessons for the public to learn to switch their preference from the car to the more efficient system. It is now best practice internationally that traffic management measures give priority to public transport, walking and cycling while restricting car movement in a city centre.

Providing a sustainable transport system for Galway is covered under a number of different transportation studies and initiatives in the last fifteen years, of which the Public Transport Feasibility Study (2009) is the most relevant as it independently analyses the city's public transport needs, based on its present and short to medium term future and planned layout.

It is noticeable that the analysis showed that the population is relatively dispersed for an urban city, that housing estates are disconnected
with few through routes suitable for public transport and that employment is largely on the fringes of the city centre and at peripheral business
parks and industrial estates. It also showed that the present public transport system has a poor image in terms of reliability, frequency, connectivity, integrated ticketing and whole journey accessibility. It identified
work and education trips as making up the vast majority of all peak period car trips. Finally, it highlighted a strong car culture in the established
employment areas of Ballybrit/Parkmore and at UCHG/NUIG and that
despite walking/cycling, being above the national average, it had reduced
in the previous twelve years, where it also noted that roundabouts in
comparison to traffic lights were a barrier to walking, cycling and public
transport systems in general. The study carried out a comparative evaluation between different transport modes based on permanence, impact
on environment, effect on travel, capacity, coverage, speed, predictabil-
ity, space, time and cost, and concluded that a public transport system
centred around lower capacity vehicles, operating at high frequency

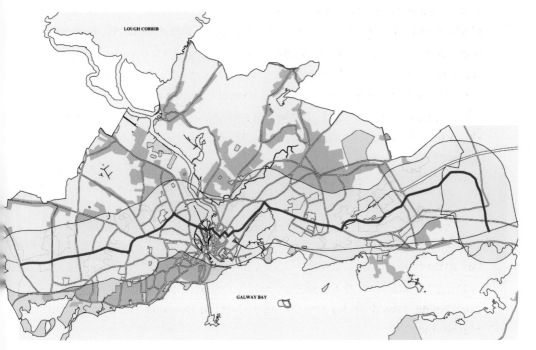

Proposed Rapid Transit Corridor

and able to penetrate residential areas was the most appropriate, given the dispersed nature of the city. Crucially, it found that because of the dispersed travel patterns, the ideal perfect network could only achieve a public transport share of 22 per cent, or 53 per cent as a total sustainable transport system, with the recommended realisable system achieving 19 per cent or 46 per cent overall.

The proposed recommended system offering the most effective and certain solution was an enhanced bus network, built around an east/ west, rapid transit corridor through the city centre, together with Park and Ride provisions at a number of 'edge of city' locations and city centre traffic management. (It did highlight that Park and Ride still involves car use and can impact on the promotion of public transport provision for commuters.) It also recommended reallocation of roads to support public transport and cycling, and the promotion of area-based travel plans for workplace, school and personalised travel planning. The Bus Rapid Transit would consist of single to triple articulated buses of 110 to 180 capacity, with an average speed of 20 kilometres per hour, running at 10 minute frequencies, similar to systems currently running in Nantes, Nancy and Eindhoven and planned for Cambridge and Luton, with potential to use hybrid vehicles with low emissions. The east/west

Proposed articulated bus for Rapid Transit Corridor

corridor through the city was the only transport corridor with sufficiently high demand to justify rapid transit, running from Ardaun on the east of the city to Ballyburke on the west and taking in the key areas of Merlin Park Hospital, GMIT, Dublin Road, City Centre, NUIG, UCHG and Western Distributor Road. Within an 800 metre catchment area or 10 minute walk, it could cater for a population currently at 50,000. The overall cost in 2009 was estimated at over €200 million and scored as medium value for money in the cost benefit analysis.

In assessing any transport proposal it is necessary to first examine the study brief – what was requested in the study and, more importantly, what was not requested. The required study was quite narrow and focussed on proposing a transport system based on the existing city and concentrated on Bus Rapid Transit or light rail to the exclusion of other possibilities. It sought proposals up to 2030 only, which was described as 'long term', and requested no input into existing or future settlement patterns. Crucially, it did not request operational and maintenance costs in addition to capital costs of the project, which is a key to the receipt of an on-going state subsidiary. Given its narrow focus, the study is a logical and practical solution to the set parameters. However, the exclusion of the main employment areas of Ballybrit and Parkmore to the east, and the major activity centre of Salthill to the west, is a major disadvantage and highlights the problem of providing an efficient transport system in a dispersed city. It also explains why the east/west linear alignment of the transit corridor runs contrary to the underlying radial pattern of the city. Whilst the extension of the Bus Rapid Transit into the future Ardaun expansion of the city improved its cost benefit analysis rating, it did not examine other settlement options that could provide similar or greater improvements. Interestingly, while it gave good examples of transport systems in other European cities and their relevant densities, it gave no equivalent density for Galway. As a consequence, the most startling finding of the study is the fairly modest 13 per cent target increase for public transport use from a very low base, on an investment of over €200 million, which again demonstrates the challenges caused by the dispersed nature of Galway's various centres of activity. In essence, Galway's present suburban settlement has insufficient density to support an alternative transport system. With an area of 2,500 hectares, it would require double its current population of 75,000 to 150,000 to be viable and more than treble, to 250,00, to be comparable to the European city norm. Even the proposed BRT corridor, covering a distance of 15 kilometres (12.5 kilometres within the city limits) with an area of 20 square kilometres and a population of 50,000 is less than half of what is required to ensure viability and just a quarter of the European city average.

It is interesting that the stated preference for the transport system in the current city development plan is still light rail, even though it comes with a price tag of €700 million and receives a poor rating in the cost benefit analysis. In a time of economic turmoil and austerity, the state's ability to invest must now be in question, which provides further problems for the city as it expands into the future. The abandonment of the Western Rail corridor extension and the removal of state subsidies to Galway Airport are local examples of a changed world. In a new age of economic surveillance and control from Europe, the state's freedom to invest in Galway's transport infrastructure will also be scrutinised. It would appear, given the new fiscal context, that Galway must now focus on creating the conditions conducive to a more extensive and effective public transport system. In essence, it must earn the right to state investment by creating a more compact and consolidated city which can support a more efficient system. In time the city council will have to take the lead and set an example in providing and promoting a sustainable transport system. This will require both the practical and symbolic gesture of gradually removing the city council staff car parking provision in preference to public transport, and the equally symbolic gesture of retiring the mayoral car as the prime mode of transport for the Mayor of Galway attending city functions. Any future public transport system for the city must be based on the journeys within the city people wish to make, rather than necessarily trying to optimise the catchment population area. Consequently, it will involve responding to the existing radial layout pattern of the city rather than just a singular linear format that maximises possible, rather than potential, users.

In anticipation of a public transport system for the city, it is necessary to first imagine moving around the city in the year 2100. That aspiration and image would see a dense and compact city similar to the historic city of Galway, with cars now excluded from the city centre and all existing multi-story car parks converted to other uses. It would see walking and cycling as the majority mode of transport within the city with bike rental available throughout the city. It would see a mass transit system as the majority mode for longer journeys, using all the existing conduits of the city with low emission car rental available for trips outside the city not covered by public transport. This type of imagining is what is required in order to determine how the city evolves from here and, crucially, what needs to be done to realise that image.

The Historic Sustainable City

The current consensus to create a more sustainable Galway is based on the notion of the historic city prior to the influence of the motor car. That ideal looks to a city that is more compact and connected, has a range of diverse uses which allow people to live, work and enjoy themselves in close proximity within an attractive urban setting and well served by

Sea Road in the historic sustainable city

187

The predominately nineteenth century Greater West area of the city

public transport – a place where people of all ages and circumstances would choose to live. That vision sees a city of neighbourhoods with a mix of use, income, age, tenure, families/household sizes and types. The best example and most appropriate model of this type of future city is the Greater West area of the city. This area, comprising sixteen hectares (forty acres) mostly dating from the nineteenth century, remains the most dense mixed, residential area outside the city centre.

Bounded by the Canal, Fr. Griffin Road, The Crescent and St. Mary's Road, the area is a typical mixed urban district containing a diverse variety of sub-areas, with a gross residential density of sixty persons per hectare, similar to what is now required to urbanise the suburban city. The area has a mix of terraced houses, apartments, shops, offices, schools, church, industry, commercial, social and health facilities. It has a mix of streets of varying types, lanes, squares, green areas, parks and canal amenities. It has a mix of families and single people, old and young and in recent years a mix of nationalities. It has a mix of middle class and working class, economically active and inactive. It has a mix of work and workers, manual, skilled and professional. It has a diverse mix of shop types, grocery, newsagent, electrical, hardware, fruit and veg, laundry, bakery, clothes, shoes, health food, locksmith, repair shop, chemist, second-hand shop and video shop. It has a mix of pubs, restaurants, coffee shops, a nightclub and music venue. It has a mix of health centre, doctor surgeries, state agencies, funeral parlour and professional offices. It has a mix of national and secondary schools, a church and convent. It has a mix of industry, large and small, garage and workshops. In summary, it is a place to live, work, shop, learn, pray and play. It is a liveable city district, where one can walk to the city centre and where traditionally one could cycle or take a tram to Salthill. It is a place where there is a sense of the pedestrian and cyclist having priority over the car, where there is a sense of enclosure, connection, streetscape and public space with a hierarchy and diversity of building types. In essence, it is a place with a sense of identity, a sense of belonging and, above all, a sense of place.

City Centre and Commercial Suburbs

The need to accommodate residential growth is the main component and primary driver of Galway City's future expansion need. Commercial development needs tend to be a consequence of that growth and are rarely the instigator of expansion. Consequently, looking at Galway's evolution for the remainder of the century will concentrate on providing homes for its growing population. However, as a result of gradually increasing demand, it is also necessary to quickly review and refer to its commercial expansion.

The city centre is still rightly seen as the main provider of the city's future commercial needs in tandem with more local neighbourhood cen-

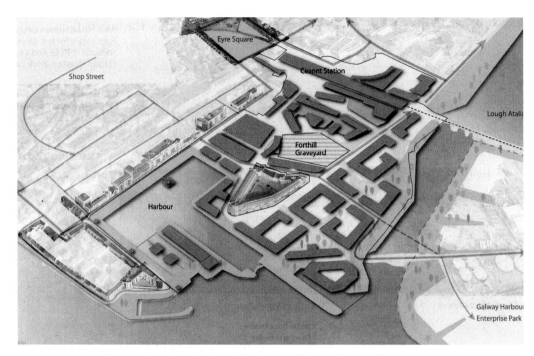

Ceannt Station/Galway Harbour – Urban Design Framework

tres. The expansion of the city centre is destined to take place in three locations – the Ceannt Station area, the Harbour area and the Inner Headford Road area. These three areas combined can provide more than double the quantity of existing commercial space in the city and can easily meet the needs of the city up to the end of the century, or up to three times its current population. All three areas are subject to more detailed urban design framework/masterplan which have been completed or are in progress. Given the current economic conditions, it is likely that any future expansion of the existing city centre will only proceed on the basis of a proper market need, so while there is an overall framework plan its implementation will be phased and, like the historical growth of the city, may tend to be organic and evolutionary in nature. The prospects and success of such large-scale expansion, as discussed earlier, will be heavily dependent on the city providing an effective and attractive public transport system to meet the demand of increasing numbers in the city centre, of which the Ceannt Station multi-transport hub will be a crucial component in conjunction with a more localised city-based system.

The existing medieval city centre, which remains the main focus and place of identity for both visitors and citizens of the city, is unlikely to change to any great extent in the future. Buildings will continue to change use, ownership or tenancy, and there will be a certain element of continuing alteration or infill development. However, given its conservation status, the general nature, form and character of the area is destined to remain relatively intact. The future expansion of the city centre around its medieval core is best seen as a surrounding, contemporary, contrast to the historic centre – a new, reinterpreted, modern expression to meet the needs and values of the twenty-first century. This will invariably result in a different feel, rather than type, of city and the location of a new optional sense of place and identity for its future inhabitants.

The fate and prospects of the existing suburban centres of commercial and other activities also need to be addressed into the future. While these centres are too diverse and dispersed to provide a coherent opinion on how they should evolve, it is noticeable that most of them are built in the landscape, rather than forming the landscape, and consequently are set back from the road boundaries rather than creating streetfronts. Every opportunity to reverse this situation needs to be pursued. The traditional urban streetscape rather than the modern suburban roadscape should be the model for the urbanisation of Galway's peripheral, edge-type developments into the future, both for existing and new neighbourhood centres. This will involve removing the provision of car parking from public view and/or reducing its need with the provision of public transport. The overall aim should be to urbanise the suburban and restore the status of the street in preference to the roadway as the primary conduit of the city.

Towards a New Approach

In addressing the future population growth of Galway and the required settlement areas to match that growth, it is necessary to take a new approach which arises out of the flawed settlement pattern of the last fifty years. That approach involves an honest assessment of its present form, density and layout to identify problem areas that need to be addressed and to formulate ways of both catering for growth and solving the deficiencies in the city. Matching growth with creating a better sense of place is the key to Galway's evolution for the remainder of the century. This approach will require a concentrated involvement from other disciplines, in particular urban design and urban economics, in conjunction with the existing planning and engineering system. It will involve looking at the city in a new, fresh and creative way, but learning from the pattern and wisdom of the historic city. It will involve challenging previously held assumptions and to correct, in an innovative way, the shortcomings of recent patterns and forms of settlement. The new approach involves three strands, as laid out below.

Information Gathering

In a desire to create a more compact and sustainable city that can support a sustainable transport system, it is necessary to go beyond the simple collation and use of hard census data, and then simply providing the predicted requirement for growth based on that data. The information gathering needs to concentrate on the existing city and, in particular, the existing suburbs. All suburban districts will require a 3D model of their neighbourhoods in order to establish an overall 3D baseline survey of the city. The survey should also include all relevant services and utilities currently not available. Beyond the physical survey, each district requires

Required 3D modelling of the city

more detailed data that goes further than the general demographics of household sizes, family types, age profiles and occupations as provided in census figures, to include the physical, social, cultural and economic issues concerning all neighbourhoods. In the context of the whole city, a detailed survey and audit of all open and recreational space is required in terms of quantity, but particularly quality, and a 3D detailed assessment is necessary under the criteria of purpose, appropriateness, usage and potential usage, improvements, redesign and reuse.

Besides a 3D physical model of the city, economic modelling is required on an on-going basis to evaluate both the existing and expanded city in relation to key elements of the infrastructure required. This is particularly needed in critical areas like public transport, public services, utilities and facilities. Further information gathering is required in respect of the future inhabitants of the expanding city. One of the major deficiencies in urban planning and design is the lack of understanding and awareness of a new generation's beliefs, attitudes and values which directly impact on how they envisage life, relationships, work, recreation, home, community and city – which in turn will influence the nature and character of urban living and how it is catered for. The final information gathering required is from the existing citizens of the city, which traditionally takes the form of submissions to the draft development plan and consequently is a reactive rather than a proactive involvement and tends to concentrate on detail rather than the overall vision for the city. A more useful mechanism would be a City Vision Online Conference within a stated timespan, where citizens of the city representing all the key social, business, cultural, design, voluntary and education sectors are invited to outline their vision for the city at the end of the twenty-first century.

Using Existing Resources

In a time of economic austerity, it is increasingly difficult to access the funds, skills and resources, particularly in light of a broader new approach to imagining the city. Consequently, it is necessary to utilise all the existing resources available to the city in order to pursue a different vision. One of the great untapped resources in Galway are the two third level institutions of NUIG and GMIT, both of which are located close to the city centre and share a deep affinity with the city. The combined student population of both colleges is 25,000 with an additional 5,000 comprising staff, post-graduate and PhD students, which is over one-third of the total population of the city. Between both institutions with their various schools, faculties and courses every conceivable aspect relevant to the city and its diverse makeup is covered, from engineering to design, from social to cultural studies, from economics to science. Currently, there is close collaboration between particular branches of the third level sector and industry in Galway, particularly in relation to IT, healthcare and energy resources. In addition, some areas of college expertise are involved at national level, including economics and law. While it is appropriate that third level colleges engage in close consultation with the future employment sector of the city, it is also important that there is engagement with the city itself. This is more than just large institutions giving something back to the city, but an acknowledgement that these institutions have resources which can have a positive effect on how their city evolves, and to which they can make a major contribution.

There is a whole host of areas where a structured, collaborative programme between the colleges and the city can reap benefits for both the city council and the citizens of the city. Most of the collaboration work would be focussed on the skills, knowledge and resources deficit of the city, and how the programme can address the deficiencies. It could involve student projects aimed at particular aspects of the city and its functions or a close student/staff liaising on various issues. It could involve staff providing expert advice or assistance on challenges facing the city or generating economic models for testing different approaches to city infrastructural works. There is probably scope in most areas of college studies that can be applied in some creative way to envisioning a future Galway.

Urban Design-led City

In the aspiration to make Galway into all the types of city it needs to be in the future – sustainable, inclusive, connected, walkable and liveable – creating a beautiful city is often forgotten. It is this ingredient more than any that people respond to and wish to experience. While the old cliché 'beauty is in the eye of the beholder' still has a certain merit, in general there are common themes that people recognise in creating an attractive and desirable city. Some of these may be subliminal, but most are still age-old, tried and tested features that have been sidelined in the last fifty years in the pursuit of a city based on function and convenience, and where for the first time in its history the scale of the human gave way to the scale of the car. The only way this can be reversed is in taking an urban design-led approach to the city where the city is shaped in a more detailed, three dimensional way. This will first involve the information gathering process and using the existing resources of the city already outlined in order to establish a more thorough picture of the existing city and a clearer, defined path for a future one. Its prime purpose, however, is to formulate the background and detailed brief for an international urban design competition that would provide the basis and blueprint for the city into the future.

Possibly titled 'Galway 2100/00', it would provide an urban design for the city up to the year 2100 to cater for a population of up to 210,000. This would be a design competition with a difference. It would be based on a 3D format for the whole city to a certain conceptual level, but not including any particular building or groups of buildings. This type of competition has not been done before in Ireland, involving a whole city, but would attract all the diverse range of current thinking on urban design as well as emerging future concepts on city living. It would encompass the key areas of settlement patterns, sustainable transport, open space, commercial hubs relative to the critical elements of density, form, overall layout and structure of the city, consistent with the unique and distinctive setting and features of Galway. It would look at addressing the change of direction the city took in the last fifty years and propose a possible new overlay on that pattern, as well as the primary question of accommodating a gradual trebling of its population during the course of the remainder of this century. Its overall challenge would be to both retain Galway's current sense of place and to develop a new sense of place for the evolving city. This type of approach would tap into the national and international awareness of Galway and hopefully engage the citizens of the city in the process, both at the formulation of the brief stage and at competition display stage. The success of a competition of this scale, scope and novelty would depend on a very clearly defined brief, arising from an unambiguous objective for the urban design exercise. This unique urban design competition would be an exciting, rewarding and revealing method of imagining Galway City in the year 2100.

Vision for the Future City

While not wishing to preempt an urban design-led proposal for Galway's future growth, it is useful to speculate on what form that growth and change could or should take in order to maintain its sense of place. This vision for Galway will look within the existing city as a genesis for its future evolvement, and generally not beyond its city boundaries, as a basis for further growth. This approach is underpinned by two important facts in regard to the city. Firstly, on the basis of a European minimum gross norm of 60 persons per hectare as now, a generally accepted requirement to create a sustainable city, Galway with an area of 50 square kilometres within its city boundaries has the potential to accommodate a population of up to 300,000 people. Secondly, the existing city, with a footprint of 25 square kilometres, has an inherent capacity to cater for 150,000 people, or double its current population. Any future vision for the city must recognise those two revealing statistics.

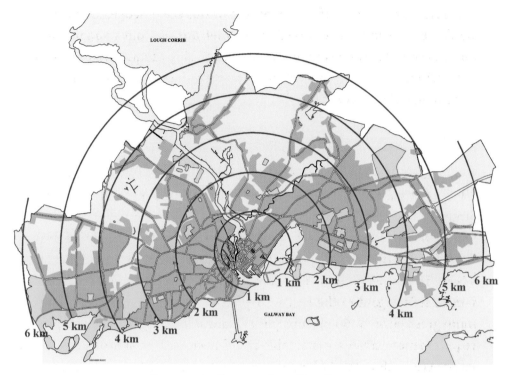

Concentric distances from Eyre Square

The other element in the vision for creating a more compact, sustainable city is one of distance from its recognised epicentre, which is the centre of Eyre Square. In an ideal scenario, the city would expand concentrically from that centre in order to maintain the minimum distance possible to its edges, which has a major impact on both identification with the city and the provision of a sustainable transport system. The exception to this is where there is an existing public transport solution which creates a linear finger effect out from the centre. However, in Galway's case this is contrary to the existing radial pattern of the city's settlement. Thus the vision for the future city concentrates on intensifying the existing city. This approach may seem radical and unnecessary. After all, within 30 minutes travel distance from Eyre Square in any direction one is in open rural countryside. The availability and extent of land is not an issue in the expansion of the city. However, sustainability based on the model of the historical city requires a new radical approach which deviates from, and in many ways is the opposite of, the last fifty years' pattern of settlement if an alternative transport system is to be facilitated and supported.

197

The creation of a more dense and compact city must be the defining vision up to the year 2100 in order to reverse the dispersal and sprawl of the last fifty years. This vision and process has three strands. Firstly, it involves consolidating and intensifying the existing suburbs, constructed in the modern period, to cater for both short and medium term population growth in the city. Secondly, it seeks to optimise whatever existing transport infrastructure is already in place and at the same time create a new, suburban village centre based on the historical model of Salthill. Finally, it looks at the historic relationship of the city with its waterways and open space as a model for providing a new type of city that is a marked departure from its proposed expansion. These three combined visionary elements, in conjunction with a relatively modest expansion of its existing footprint, can cater for the city's growth up to the end of the century and provide the ingredients for a viable, cost effective and sustainable transport system as well as maintain and enhance its sense of place.

The Roofhome City

The concept of the Roofhome City involves inhabiting the roof or air space over the existing low density suburbs of the city to create a new upper level of habitation. This approach would immediately open up the possibility of catering for population growth within the city, when it starts to occur again, in the areas that have a low and ageing population, in larger, low occupancy house units than are now required to address the rapidly changing demographics of the city. This idea recognises that the existing homes and neighbourhoods are already clearly established, both legally and physically, in terms of site boundaries, road access and open space. Consequently, this type of intensification of the city is likely to be more piecemeal or phased, rather than a comprehensive and complete redevelopment of the existing suburbs. Therefore, the possibility of an on-going variation in height can add rather than detract, which is consistent with the existing tradition of visual diversity within the historic city. This type of consolidation and density increase could only proceed on the basis of a comprehensive study and 3D local area plan for each existing suburban district, which would clearly identify the opportunities and potential of each neighbourhood for intensification, connectivity, diversity, variety,

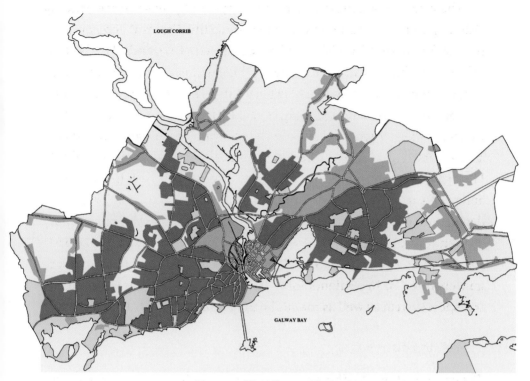

Extent of Roofhome City

efficiency and adaptability, plus environmental improvements to the public realm.

Each neighbourhood is likely to reveal different challenges and opportunities, resulting in a variety of design solutions across the suburbs, with no single blanket proposal likely to emerge to suit all conditions. However, in most cases it would result in a vertical rather than a horizontal increased density because of established access and legal boundaries. The immediate visual impact of the approach would be the gradually raising of the height of the existing suburbs from two to a new four story base height, which would change the characteristics of the existing settlement pattern from a suburban to a more urban scale, and create a better sense of enclosure and streetscape within individual existing neighbourhoods. The study would also identify any brownfield sites within the area which are suitable for regeneration, and any proposed alterations to existing open space to improve its amenity value. The proposed Roofhome City would likely encourage individual plot, rather than multiple plot,

Time to Grow Up!

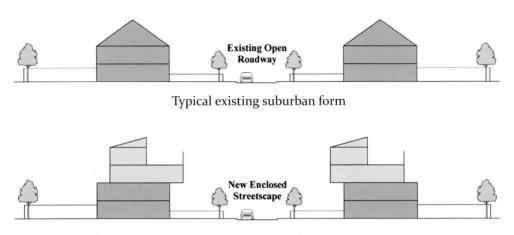

Typical existing suburban form

Proposed refurbia

Suburban renewal – Conceptual Roofhome City

development and, because of the nature of the vertical expansion and the proximity to existing homes, would likely favour off-site, dry, pre-fabricated construction which would ensure higher quality with greater control, particularly in relation to ecological and energy elements.

The mandatory and simultaneous upgrading of the existing ground-based home to modern energy standards would ensure overall combined efficiencies in terms of density and energy usage. Because it would be a new approach to achieving greater density in the overall city, it is difficult to predict supply and demand. However, given that Galway is coming to the end of a first generation of users to experience city apartment living, this is a logical next step to a new, related type of home ownership located in established suburbs. It is also an appropriate model for the new reduced and defined 'family' type that is evolving in Galway, and an acceptance that city centre family living is still another generation or two away in that evolutionary process.

The Seafront Railway City

The Seafront Railway City seeks to combine and optimise two aspects of the existing city which to date have not been explored or exploited. The first element is the existing railway line, which flanks the eastern shore of the city and which, uniquely in Ireland, terminates at the recognised heart of the city at Eyre Square. The second is the eastern seafront of the city which remains generally hidden, unknown and undeveloped, despite enjoying an extensive seashore amenity, including a beach area onto Galway Bay. As a piece of transport infrastructure, the railway line is an invaluable asset to the city. The proposal to twin track the existing line to Athenry, as well as providing a new, multi-modal passenger ter-minal in Ceannt Station, linking rail and bus services, though on hold at the moment due to the economic situation, has the potential to greatly enhance rail access to Galway. This improved rail facility has generally been seen as an option only for commuters into the city on the mainline train service, and those travelling from Athenry, or from the proposed new railway station at Oranmore. However with twin tracking, it has the

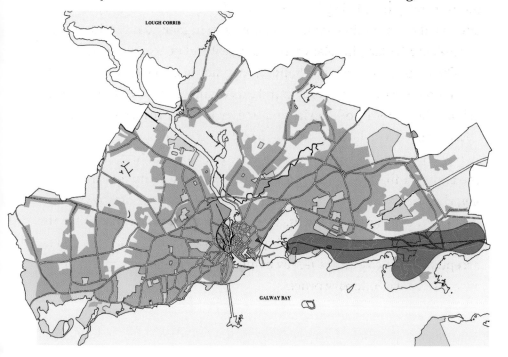

Extent of Seafront Railway City

Seafront Railway City

potential to provide a Dart-like service from the eastern bayside suburbs of the city into the city centre.

To render that service viable would require a concentrated spine of density on or around the route of the line on the eastern side of the city, consistent with the internationally established concept of higher densities on main transport corridors. Indeed, Galway already has an appropriate model for that type of seafront development in the western side of the city, namely the popular and traditional resort village of Salthill. This area, with a density of 1.75, is the only suburban centre in Galway which enjoys an almost comparable density to the city centre, and is a useful example for a similar dense village on the east seafront suburb which could exploit both the beach and surrounding amenities of Balyloughan strand and the adjacent rail link into the city. The regeneration of the eastern coastal suburb would also involve the potential to incorporate land areas that are either currently underutilised or no longer appropriate. In that regard, Renmore barracks may fit into that category. Its relocation would form part of the overall evolution and consolidation of defence and military activities in Ireland and free the area to form part of the eastern village spine of the city. The vision of a dense village along the coastal railway line is very much contrary to the current, more open recreational or low density proposal for the general area. However, that proposal of retreating from the water is alien to both the historic city of Galway and the resort village of Salthill, where a very strong and coherent built edge to the water not only defined but helped emphasise the amenity of the bay.

The contemporary trend to provide a recreational edge rather than a building edge loses that historic, traditional feature of containment and visual support evident in the old city. Indeed, the more recent fashion for providing open park areas, adjacent to the sea, as represented by the series of green protrusions into the bay along Salthill promenade, dilutes the vital visual relationship between the pedestrian viewer and the sea and provides an incongruous element in the highly exposed, coastal seafront. This is evident in the numerous open spaces in Salthill which are completely underutilised due to the more appealing attraction of the 'promenade' walk. The proposed Seafront Railway City is therefore a considered response to the untapped potential of the existing railway line and the desire to create a new Salthill Village on the eastern side of the coastal city which would accommodate a linear promenade, rather than a static park area, more appropriate to its exposed location.

The Riverfront 'Green' City

The Riverfront 'Green' City invokes the spirit and memory of the city, not just back to its birth, but to the earliest settlers in Mesolithic times. This vision for a new settlement uses the meandering route of the River Corrib as both the orientating and access element to a new 'Green' city, which would stretch from the city centre to Lough Corrib. Thus the new riverfront edge of habitation, physically and symbolically, connects the city to the lake, in the same way the River Corrib links them naturally. The new resultant axis would radically re-orientate the city in a new direction. Instead of expanding east and west, parallel to its coastal sea edge, the city would for the first time extend northwards from its historic core to Lough Corrib, creating a new north/south city axis. The new axis would reflect both the first settler route north from the city and the long subsequent history of the River Corrib, which provided the conduit for

Extent of Riverfront 'Green' City

people, trade and later recreation in connecting the lake to Galway Bay and Corrib County to the city. It also symbolically connects the historic, walled town to the oldest known structure in the city, that of the Megalithic tomb on the shore of Lough Corrib, north of Menlo.

The concept of creating a 'Green' sustainable settlement, in the purest sense of the word, has a number of background elements. Firstly, the existing river bank lands have relatively poor access in terms of a road network. Part of the lands are proposed for conservation designation, although that does not preclude some form of usage and even that general designation policy is under question at the moment. Galway is partially seen as an alternative city, where alternative views and lifestyles are both prevalent and part of the city's cultural mix. The traditional indigenous villages at both the lake and sea estuary ends of the river, consisting of the Claddagh and Menlo settlements, could both in today's terms be described as models of sustainability in terms of lifestyles, including home and shelter, food and sustenance, clothing and footwear, transport and mobility. Invoking rather than replicating that model is the vision for the Riverfront 'Green' City. The vision sees it as a generally car-less city, where the river itself provides the watery highway, the passive designed homes would require no conventional heating other than back-up district heating, and where insulation and renewals are brought to a new experimental level of innovation. The reward for such an alternative way of living, and an exemplar in sustainability, is the amenity value of the river, a proximity to the city centre and a low cost lifestyle.

Similar to the Seafront Railway City, the vision for the Riverfront 'Green' City challenges current assumptions in regard to open space, particularly as it relates to the extensive waterways and water bodies of the city. Presently the banks of the River Corrib are seen as a long, linear, passive parkland area, with little usage and access, which is contrary to the historic city which embraces the river in a very immediate way. That deference to the river is both unnecessary and self-defeating, and fails to recognise that it is the river itself that is the amenity attraction which needs to be accessed and positively exploited. The current position, where vast banks of the river within walking distance of Eyre Square are retained as green space with an insufficient population to support it, creating a pastoral, rural setting adjacent to the city core, is both misguided and

The Riverfront 'Green' City

The river as potential transport route within the city

contrary to the idea of encouraging an urban mindset. This ill-conceived approach of providing amorphous green areas along waterways merely confirms the faults of the last fifty years of modern planning's inability to create open space that is contained, concentrated, accessible, usable, viable and supportable by a surrounding population – open space that is based on quality rather than quantity and that learns from the historic models of the old city. In principle, this involves providing a strong built edge to waterways, to both emphasise and exploit the appeal of water and where green, open space is generally more important in areas removed from the attraction of water.

Cultural City

Galway's cultural credentials are well established at this stage, although most notably confined to the performance area. The visual arts continues to take a backseat, both in terms of exposure and space provision. The notion of Galway as the bilingual capital of the Gaeltacht also adds to this cultural association. However, the idea of Galway as a cultural city is somewhat overstated and more of a branding and marketing exercise than a clear recognisable exception in comparison to other Irish cities. What is irrefutable is that its three nationally and internationally known cultural brands – the Druid Theatre Company, Galway Arts Festival and Macnas – have placed Galway at the cutting edge of the cultural and arts community, with a well established reputation for innovation, inventiveness and quality. All three cultural forces emerged from the alternative, left bank environment of 1970s and 1980s, and over thirty years later now find themselves part of the national and even international arts establishment. The challenge for all three is to continually reinvent themselves in order to remain relevant, as the journey always tends to be more exciting than the arrival.

During that evolutionary period, it was always going to be difficult for other cultural seeds in the city to bear fruit in what was a high standard of activity on a highly competitive stage. It is also relevant that all three cultural brand names were born and nurtured in barren recessionary Galway, where time, space and a certain impoverishment proved more beneficial for cultivation than the later urgencies of economic prosperity. As the city reverts to its previous state of economic struggle and difficulty, it may, ironically, prove to be a more fertile breeding ground for a

The Town Hall Theatre

The Taibhdhearc Theatre

new era of cultural forces to emerge. Will the city now recognise and support new potential? Will new talent prepare to risk itself in a crowded cultural environment, now leaden with a recent arts tradition which invites comparison and criticism? Are there new patrons and benefactors, similar to Druid's experience in their occupation of a donated venue? Galway's continued cultural evolvement will be dependent on the answers to these questions. The future of Galway as a cultural city must also be viewed against the context of its, and indeed the country's, cultural reputation as a source and means to economic recovery. Could Galway, for example, present and brand itself as Ireland's City of Culture in the same way Limerick wishes to sell itself as Ireland's City of Sport, based on its record, tradition and reputation?

There is no doubt that culture sells – cultural tourism is the fastest growing category in the sector. Galway is a living example of that, where the annual Arts Festival, Macnas parade and a host of other cultural festivals are major contributors to the city's coffers. Galway's vibrant arts scene is also dependent on its ability to sell in order to survive and flourish. The city benefits economically from both obvious and subtle cultural associations, images, attributes and impressions. Indeed, Galway's cultural creativity is also helpful in attracting inward business investment as it suggests a climate of innovation and intuitive thinking, a place where ideas are nurtured and encouraged. However, the formal branding of Galway as a Cultural City could be a step too far as a marketing initiative, because it would ultimately end up diminishing and destroying the creativity that it wishes to promote. Culture and commerce can and do coexist, provided each are allowed the freedom to first evolve and develop independently. Artistic and cultural endeavour is a natural, organic process, with no defined or predictable source or growth. Trying to cultivate it within a formal cultural system is akin to trying to create a genetically modifiable product, which is alien to the artistic and cultural journey. Consequently, Galway as a potential city of culture must continue to simply remain open, amenable and supportive of new possibilities and emerging artistic innovation.

Tourist City

Tourism continues to be one of the largest economic sectors in Galway and the sector that is now most identified with the city. Approximately two million tourists visit Galway each year, comprising both domestic and international visitors, predominantly from Great Britain, continental Europe and North America. It is a complex sector covering a multiplicity of tourist types, categories and headings. These categories include such data as visitor numbers, visitor spend, visitors by month, origin, route and method of entry, purpose of visit, type of holiday, composition of party, age, gender, social class, duration of stay, type of internal transport and accommodation type. In general, Galway's tourist types

Salthill Beach and Promenade

can be broken down into festival tourists, cultural tourists, event tourists, excursion tourists, shopping tourists, casual/social tourists, family tourists, weekend tourists and study tourists. The physical impact of the growing tourist market is a constantly evolving city, as it shapes itself to service the visitor market. This is reflected in the ever changing range of accommodation, hospitality, retail and cultural provisions in the city. Surprisingly, it has not resulted in any central, indoor dedicated visitor centre as provided in the other main cities in Ireland.

The vast majority of tourists to the city are still drawn to the relatively small historic city centre, which remains the main attraction for most visitors. The compactness and intimacy of the area, combined with the volume and flow of visitors, further emphasises the bustling and vibrant nature of the medieval core. However, the sheer numbers and success of Galway's tourist sector is a double-edged sword. The volume of visitors is indirectly impacting on the unique holiday experience they seek. In the high tourist season, visitors can outnumber residents by two to one, which tends to remove the sense of local from its locality and denies the visitors the authenticity of a city rooted in its indigenous and everyday life. In short, visitors get to see the city inhabited by other visitors. It is also impacting on the character of the city itself, as gradually local indigenous shops and businesses are replaced by national and international multiples and brand names, changing its nature to an 'anywhere city'. Thus, Galway's city centre is gradually providing a universal experience, somewhat packaged and in danger of becoming a medieval stage set, catering for visitors rather than a local, living and breathing city that simply accommodates visitors.

Ironically, one of the causes of this drift from its roots is also one of its success stories – the gravitational pull of its pedestrian spine from Eyre Square down Shop Street to the Fishmarket, where the vast concentration of visitors congregate. To address this, Galway needs to expand its visitor attractions in order to disperse numbers over a larger number of tourist focus areas in the city. To a certain extent the regeneration of Ceannt Station, the Inner Harbour area and Inner Headford Road area will help to bring more diversity to the city centre and help dissipate the crowded pedestrian spine. However, all these regeneration projects are large-scale, long-term projects which will be subject to market conditions. The city also needs to look at more small-scale, environmental improvement-type projects. In addition, the city needs to pursue other areas removed from the city centre, as a means of dispersing visitors to other city attractions. There are three potential locations for such work, two in the city centre and one in the western coastal suburbs, which can help alleviate the compressed nature of the oldest part of the city. All three initiatives will require a thorough analysis of what is required and a vision to realise that requirement. The following is a quick summary of the three and a general outline of what can be aspired to.

Dominick Street/O'Brien's Bridge

Dominick Street Lower is one of the finest streets in the city with its nineteenth century streetscape still essentially intact. In recent years it has become the new 'left bank' of the city, which is appropriate given its west bank location, isolated from the existing city core and increasingly the night-time cafe and culinary centre of the city, with a diverse range of restaurants and eating establishments. O'Brien's Bridge is the middle bridge of the three historic, stone bridge crossings of the River Corrib

Dominick Street as suitable setting for pedestrianisation

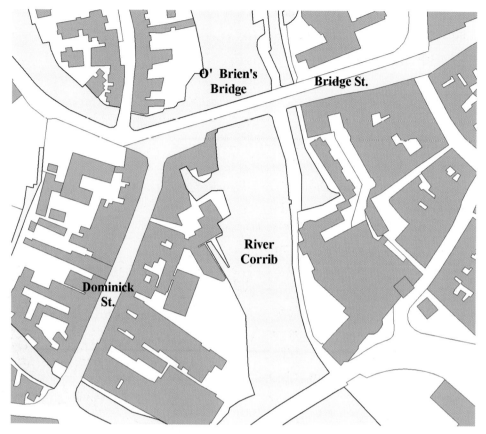

Dominick Street pedestrianisation

and the one that most connects the east and west, older parts of the city. With the introduction of the one-way traffic system in the city in the 1980s, the carrying capacity of the bridge is now just half of the two other traditional bridges.

The proposed vision for this area is the removal of vehicular traffic from Dominick Street Lower and the south side of O'Brien's Bridge and to extend the pedestrianisation of the city centre across half of the bridge surface and over all of Dominick Street Lower. This will effectively link the east and west of the river and city by connecting Mainguard Street to Dominick Street, via the bridge, and expand the focus of visitors to the new pedestrian street. Dominick Street can then fully capitalise on its culinary status within the city by extending its cafe culture onto the street and create a new ambient street culture in this area of high potential and promise.

Woodquay/Corrib Terrace

Woodquay and Corrib Terrace combined is a linear, elongated section of unexploited open space, stretching from Daly's Place to the River Corrib and bisected by the heavily traf-ficked Headford Road. All of the Woodquay side of the divided open space is a hard surface of a gradually widening streetscape, with a central island of surface car parking. The Corrib Ter-race end of the area is mainly a railed-in, park area with some adjoining surface car parking. The character of the general dis-trict is essentially a small-scale mixture of commercial and resi-dential uses with a local area feel

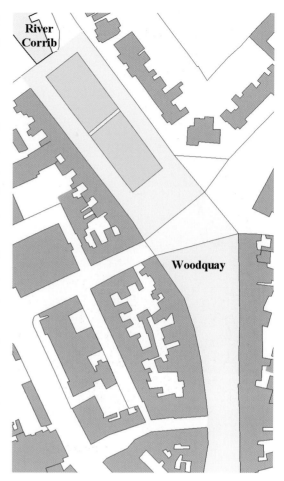

Woodquay Precinct

to it. With the exception of the park at Corrib Terrace, the area is very much dominated by traffic and surface parking.

Similar to the Dominick Street area, the proposed vision for Wood-quay and Corrib Terrace is the removal of the surface car parking and the reduction of the road area in order to maximise the pedestrianisation of the area. It is important that both areas are seen as part of the same pe-destrian environment in order to physically and visually connect Wood-quay to the River. This will involve removing the railings from around the park at Corrib Terrace and allow the green area to form part of the new pedestrian floor to the overall open space. The primary objective of the project is to improve the visual environment, create a new pedestrian

Corrib Terrace and Woodquay open space changes

precinct in what was originally a market area of the city, to encourage small-scale habitation of the open space and form another focus for visitors to the city.

Extended Salthill Seafront Area

Salthill was once the popular and traditional holiday resort village of Galway, combining the peculiarly Irish ingredients of beach, hotel, resort shop, amusement arcade and ballroom. Gradually, its popularity waned as holiday makers sought more predictable foreign climates, leading to the gradual change from holiday accommodation to apartments. Now it is essentially a suburban village centre, serving the western coastal environs of the city. However, it still retains its magnificent aspect onto Galway Bay and the ever popular promenade walk. Today, while the physical village is still intact and identifiable, the promenade walk is now much more extensive, and effectively the seafront amenity of Salthill now stretches from South Park, near the city, to beyond Salthill Golf Club at Knocknacarra. This whole stretch has been subject to a successive range of ad hoc changes and interventions over the last fifty years, which has resulted in an incoherent and car-dominated waterfront. As a result, it now has a tired and jaded appearance and, with the loss of the holiday resort business, Salthill needs to reinvent itself in order to exploit the still powerful amenity of its seafront and become a magnet for a new wave of visitors.

The proposed vision for the area centres on redefining the relationship between people and vehicles, and to overcome its primary problem, that of the pedestrian competing for the amenity of the bay with the car, whether road traffic or car parking. In terms of the village area itself, it involves reforming the road network and reducing car parking in order to increase the public realm and provide a buffer between pedestrian and vehicular movement. The prom area extending to South Park involves a far more radical proposal, consisting of the realignment of Grattan Road and Seafront Promenade to form a new street frontage and reversing the location of Claude Toft Park, the children's playground and adjoining open spaces directly onto the Prom seafront. This would provide a new, linear, green, pedestrian zone from South Park to Salthill Park, separated and removed from passing traffic and car parking. The proposal will

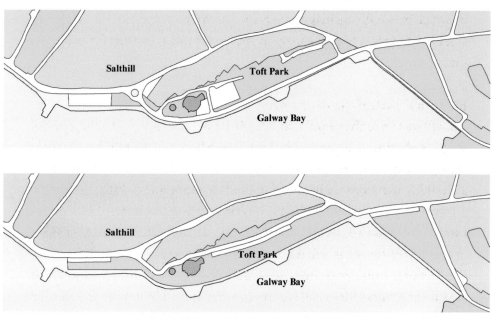

Existing Salthill Seafront (top) and
proposed Salthill Seafront (bttom)

Walking Salthill Prom on the way to 'kicking the wall'

greatly enhance the amenity of the prom walk, allow for the development of further public seafront amenity buildings and act as a catalyst for diverting visitors from the city centre area.

The Home and Neighbourhood

The home, as the base unit of the future city, and the neighbourhood, as the base unit of the communal city, will require particular attention if the city is to reconnect with its sense of place as created in the historic city. In many ways the home and neighbourhood are destined to undergo a fundamental change in character from that provided in the last fifty years. Of these, the home is likely to see the greatest change from the traditional unit. It is one of the ironies in the growth and expansion of the suburbs in the last half century that little evolution took place in both the design and construction of the home. The house, during that period, maintained a traditional format, where the only evolution was superficial in nature. So while the external skin may have gone through a range of treatments, the site and floor plan remained generally constant and traditional. The future changes in home design and construction are likely to be driven by a number of factors.

The current economic turmoil in the country may impact on both the mobility and home ownership rates of a public seeking certainty in a fearful environment. The gradual reduction of home occupancy rates, towards the European norm, will influence the form and character of supply in a changing market. But the biggest change is likely to be driven by the current trend towards passive house design, where houses will be required to optimise their design sustainability in order to maximise energy usage set at a very challenging threshold. This is likely to bring about the most radical changes in designing the homes of tomorrow. It may usher in a completely new aesthetic, as houses embrace all the elements and apparatus of passive house systems and technology, where the traditional open fire and open window give way to a new airtight and controlled insulated environment, without the need for a conventional heating system other than a minimum backup. This will result in higher construction and upfront costs, but lower maintenance and operational costs. It is also likely to change the traditional method of on-site wet construction to off-site dry construction in order to meet the much higher standards of workmanship and quality control required with regulated passive house design.

In terms of neighbourhoods, much more emphasis will be placed on high quality, urban design and architecture to create distinctive environments and foster good community relationships. The emphasis in future neighbourhoods will be on layouts that develop a distinguishing sense of place, well connected, with good variety, that provide people friendly streets and spaces, which make the most efficient use of resources and create a safe and enjoyable public realm. The new higher required densities, accompanied by smaller lower occupancy houses, will invariably lead to more terraced, duplex or apartment block arrangements, with minimum scope for individualism. This more democratic approach will be more suitable and amenable to a mix of use, tenure, income, age and family compositions than the previous low density segregated suburbs of the last fifty years. Overall, the future neighbourhoods of the city will be places where people will satisfy their daily needs, close to amenities, facilities and services, well connected with transport links to employment, shopping and leisure and have a strong historical, cultural and visual connection to the city.

City Twinning

City twinning is a process where two cities agree to form a relatively loose but formal arrangement of contact and co-operation in the political, social, economic or cultural areas. The concept has a long tradition, but became more popular in Europe in the wake of both world wars as cities with similar war experiences shared and assisted each other in a common history of devastation, survival and rebuilding after the war. In the more recent past, the bonds have become more tenuous as the reasons for twinning became less clear, other than a notional sharing of common interests, whether in the educational, employment or cultural spheres. Today, city twinning has become somewhat debased, with some cities twinning with over twenty other cities, of which the citizens would probably struggle to name more than one or two of them. For some sceptics, it merely represents a junket or free holiday for the relevant dignitaries of both cities and has no longer any useful purpose.

Galway City is officially twinned with 11 other cities worldwide. These cities include five in the USA and one each in England, Canada, France, New Zealand, Denmark and China, which in many ways highlights the city's cultural preferences. While the benefits of large-scale city twinning are dubious, there is a case for cities that are pursuing an imagined type of future and wish to learn from the experiences of other cities pursuing a similar vision. In Galway's case the idea of seeking an appropriate twin in terms of a sustainable, compact city with a similar population and projected growth by the end of the century could be a very informative use of the twinning function.

One such possibility is the city of Freiburg in south-western Germany, generally regarded as the world's green capital city of sustainability. With a population of 225,000, it has similar characteristic to Galway in terms of age and origin, a university town and gateway city to the scenic Black Forest region. However, it is its green credentials, including higher densities and an efficient public transport system, that Galway can learn from. In the absence of such a twinning becoming a reality there are numerous other similar sized cities in both Holland and Sweden, two other countries with strong experience of sustainable cities, which could be pursued in order for Galway to obtain an appropriate match and help to connect Galway back to its historic European source and roots.

City Image

A city's image is how outsiders or visitors generally perceive it, irrespective of how that city portrays or presents itself. In Galway's case, the city unofficially brands itself in different ways at different times, including Tourist City, Cultural City, Maritime City, Gaelic City, IT City, Healthcare City, Festival City or City of Learning. However, viewed from the outside, the most common perception of the city in general commentary, both subtle and direct, is that of a Party City. That perception pervades the whole visitor and observer sector of Galway, ranging from both print and broadcast media, tourist guides and social media, to domestic and international visitor experience and opinion. To a large extent that image was gradually created and nurtured by an expanding festival calendar, rendering Galway the festive capital of Ireland, combined with a bustling pub environment, a vibrant music scene, an ambient street culture and a youthful, energetic student population. The irony, of course, is that for many typical residents who go about their daily lives the image of Party City is more curious than credible, and does not accurately reflect the reality of living in the city.

Like most city images, Galway's is essentially just skin deep. Generally, its importance therefore is both superficial and transitory. However, in a tourist city like Galway image takes on a greater significance, as visitors tend to base their decision to visit particular cities on its general perception and image. For Galway, therefore, the concept of Party City, though very successful at present, carries a certain level of discomfort and uncertainty. The idea of Galway being the release valve for the country suggests a city whose main function is to provide a base for a national party and associated hangover. The concern is that parties are fragile, temporary experiences, as party-goers constantly seek new locations to indulge their shared pursuit of enjoyment and craic. The other concern is that party cites are not taken seriously, as the predominant image is based on conviviality and frivolity. The final issue is that Galway's brand as Party City'may be concealing all the other features and attractions that the city has to offer for visitors. In general, it is very difficult for a city to alter or modify its image even if it wanted to, once it is embedded in the consciousness of observers and visitors. Galway's particular festival, social and cultural mix is its most defining and observed inhabited trademark. Over time the brand will tend to evolve, mutate or dissipate.

One potential morphing of the current image into a future version that the city could pursue is the idea of a creative city. The creative should come with a small c, in that it is not a self-proclaimed title, just a simple approach to tackling all the elements and issues of the city in a creative way. It is based on the fact that the city is currently a culturally creative city, where the arts are seen as its most creative endeavour in terms of output and quality. The seeping of that creativity into all other areas of Galway life, from the most mundane and banal to the most prominent

and exotic, is a worthwhile and visionary recipe for its future life. The city council can be both the instigator and inspiration for such creativity by adopting an original and innovative approach to the city's future growth and change. However, there is no reason why that creativity could not extend to all aspects of Galway's life and makeup, including its employment, education, commercial, leisure and other sectors. The change from Party City to Creative City would be an on-going, organic process, at times silent, at times vocal, which would require the 'establishment' city to embrace the idea in order to deliver the more creative city of the future.

A Sense of Place – Summary

Galway's unique sense of place is defined by its diverse range of waterways, regularly topped up by its equally watery climate, its built form in native limestone as its core construction material and by successive inhabitation by a series of foreigners who left their distinctive imprint on the city from the thirteenth to the twenty-first centuries. That distinguishing sense of place is generally identified and confined to the historic, older part of the city, the core which is seen as embodying the essence of the city. Consequently, its centre is the main focus for both citizens and visitors to the city in seeking to connect with the idea of urban life in all its attributes and associations. Thus, the Anglo-Norman and later Anglo-Irish built city has become the predominantly visible stage on which the city's commercial, social, cultural and celebratory life is acted out. The pedestrianisation of the city core has helped to expose and reveal the organic informality and intimacy of the medieval city and its nineteenth century overlay. Therefore, it's sense of place and likability as a city is expressed in that distinctive mix of the physical city, with layers from the medieval to the modern, the nature of its human activity by residents and visitors, its diverse uses, ranging from social to economic, all against the backdrop of its various water attractions.

However, Galway is now a divided city with the compact historic centre separated from its surrounding, dispersed periphery by the character and scale of both. The perceived city centre, at around 25 hectares, now represents only 1 per cent of the total footprint of the city of 2,500 hectares. The vast periphery, though only created in the last fifty years, now dwarfs the small centre formed in the previous 700 years, fuelled by the recent modern trends of urbanisation and industrialisation. These suburbs, now the dominant area and settlement pattern of the city, consisting of a mix of low density housing and various centres of economic activity that was once the domain of the city core, is a product of the new consumerist and individualist society of the past half century. While the historic city had Anglo-Norman origins and was based on the European tradition of cities, the suburbs are Anglo-American in origin and based on that hybrid form. Thus Galway today is a split Euromerican city with a European style centre and an American style edge.

It is natural to be drawn to the old part of medieval Galway, its patina of age, its sense of successive textures of history and all the quirks, curiosities and accidents of urbanism that are on display. It is also easy to be sentimental about the later Anglo-Irish historic city, given that it didn't have to confront the three great city altering forces of the second half of the twentieth century – the car, large-scale urban expansion and a social/cultural revolution – even though dense areas of nineteenth century Galway still remain an appropriate model of urban life that could have accommodated all three forces. Indeed, the car and all its cultural trappings of convenience and materialism had as much impact, by stealth, on Galway than war and its associated devastation had on European cities during both world wars. Consequently, while the city centre represents its sense of place, the suburbs now represents its loss of place.

Ironically, this duality coincided with the concept of the controlled, planned city in the modern era, as distinct from the natural, organic city in the historic era. The historic city was characterised by invention and informality, the modern city by uniformity and conformity. The paradox of the highly regulated present and generally unregulated past is the reality that some of the present icons of Galway City such as St. Nicholas' Church, Lynch's Castle and Spanish Arch would probably fail to comply with the current objectives and policies of planning control. The drift from an urban type city to a suburban one was primarily due to particular social, economic, cultural circumstances and influences, particularly Anglo-American ones. However, defects in the general approach to city planning, including an inadequate timeframe for future growth and an overly narrow input and mindset, resulted in the gradual erosion of the urban spirit and memory of the city. Today, Galway endures all the challenges posed by suburban sprawl, particularly in relation to an ability to support a sustainable transport system as a viable alternative to the motor car, which increasingly is creating major traffic problems, particularly to the east of the city and compounded by the fact that geographically Galway is susceptible to being choked by vehicular traffic. Galway also has an existing structural deficit, in that its current settlement pattern of three Ds – dispersal, decentralisation and deurbanisation – is unable to support a viable transport system which is also based on three Ds – that of density, which determines usage; distance, which decides frequency; and demarcation, which influences speed. Galway's low density settlement and land use pattern of the last fifty years is now the main contributor to its current traffic problems, and is also the main obstacle to solving them in the form of a transport system, whether personal (walking/cycling) or public (bus/tram/train/boat).

The vision for its future growth, expansion and change is based on learning from its nineteenth century built heritage – a dense, liveable city with the option of an alternative transport use. In preference to further expanding the city eastwards towards its effective connection to Oranmore, it outlines a three-pronged approach to consolidating and intensifying the existing city, based on increasing the density of existing suburbia, creating a new dense spine on its sole existing transport infrastructure and renewing its historical association with water and open space. That process will urbanise suburbia and help revert the city back toward the density it had fifty years ago and to the scale of the human, rather than the scale of the car. This will require taking a 3D urban design-led approach to Galway, including an urban design competition and utilising the full resources of the city, in particular a collaborative engagement between the city and its third level institutions. In doing so the city is borrowing from its cultural creativity to connect back to its European roots as the appropriate model for creating a compact, sustainable city, a city where its sense of place is not just confined to its core, but carries out to its surrounding periphery to heal the split and discrepancy between the perceived city at its centre and the ignored city at its edge.

In these strange economic times and subtle cultural and demographic shifts in the city, this frugal and measured approach to correct the fundamental, structural and visual deficit in the city is ironically the right concept in the right place at the right time to achieve the right outcome. Galway in the year 2100, with a potential population of 210,000, needs to be imagined with an overall and not just partial sense of place, if it is to fully embrace the full title, Galway – A Sense of Place.

BIBLIOGRAPHY

Hardiman's History of Galway (1820) J. Hardiman

Old Galway (1983) M.D. O'Sullivan

Galway 1790–1914 (2004) J. Cunningham

The History of Galway (1999) S. Spellissy

Discover Galway (2001) P. Walsh

Galway in Stone (2002) M. Feely

Galway's Heritage in Stone (2007) Galway City Council

Some Galway Memories (1981) M. Semple

Galway Architectural Heritage (1985) W. Garner

Vanishing Galway (1987) P. O'Dowd

The Corrib County (1993) R. Hayward

Stone Buildings (1998) P. Mc Afee

Exploring Ireland's Historic Towns (2010) P. Dargan

Atlas of the Irish Rural Landscape (2003) F. Aalen, K. Whelan, M. Stout

Urban Environments (2001) E. Mapelli

The New Housing 2 (2009) R.I.A.I

Galway City Development Plan (2011–2017) Galway City Council

Galway Public Transport Feasibility Study (2009) M.V.A Consultancy

Galway Transportation and Planning Study (1999) C. Buchanan & Partners

Development Plan Guidelines (2007) Department of the Environment

INDEX

Aalto, Alva, 89
American Power Corporation, 28
Anglo-Normans, 21–23, 141
Aran Islands, 4, 6
Atlantaquarium, 8
Augustine Church, 26
Augustinians, 26
Avaya, 28

Baboró Festival, 31, 106
Barnacle, Nora, 125
Bechman Coulter, 28
Bioware, 28
Black Box Theatre, 106
Blake's Castle, 52, 75, 98
Blake's Tower, 21
Blakes, 22
Boston Scientific, 28
Browne's Doorway, 96
Bruen, Ken, 125
Bus Rapid Transit, 185–6
Byrne, R., 88

Capuchins, 25
Carmelites, 25
Ceannt Station, 178, 190, 201
Cisco, 28

Cistercians, 25, 83
city twinning, 218–9
Claddagh, the, 6, 7, 14, 26,
    56–60, 64, 97, 100, 204
Claddagh Ring, 58, 143
Claude Toft Park, 215
Colahan, Arthur, 6
College Showgrounds, 114
Columbus, Christopher, 98
conduits, 168–9, 187, 191, 203
Connacht Rugby Team, 113
Connemara, 14, 29, 33
Cookes Thatched Pub, 117
Corinthians, 113
Corrib Terrace, 213–4
Courthouse, 85–6, 99
Crane Bar, 117
Cromwellian siege, 21–2, 24, 27,
    52
Crosby, Bing, 6
Cúirt International Festival, 31,
    106
Cullen, T.J., 88
Cultural City, 206–9
Cusack, J., 87

D'Arcys, 22

Deacy, Eamon 'Chick', 113

'Dead, The', xix

de Burgo, Richard, 19–21

density, 57, 62–6, 150, 152–4, 158–64, 171, 174, 176–8, 182, 185, 189, 191, 195, 198–200, 202–3, 217, 222–3

development plans, 66, 154–8, 160, 177

Development Plans – Guidelines for Local Authorities, 155

Digital Equipment Corporation, 27

Docks, 98–9

Dominican Church, 36

Dominican Nuns, 26

Dominicans, 26

Dominick Street, 53–4, 102, 124, 211–3

Druid Theatre, 98, 106, 108, 207

Early Music Festival, 31

Eglinton Canal, 4, 14–15

Eglington Pier, 100

Eglington, Lord, 14

Els Comediants, xviii, 110

Eyre family, 24

Eyre Square, 24, 53–5, 95–6, 169, 197, 201

   fountain, 93, 130

Eyre Square Shopping Centre, 71, 75

Fianna Fáil, 138

Fidelity, 28

Finn, Alec, 117

Fishmarket, 76, 97–8

Foster, Thomas, 60

Franciscan Abbey, 26, 54, 85, 87

Franciscans, 26

Gaelic settlements, 57–60

Galvia, 2, 9

Galway Arts Festival, 106, 109, 207

Galway Bay, 4–8, 103, 140, 162, 169, 201, 204, 214

Galway Bay Sailing Club, 13

Galway Cathedral, 27, 56, 90–1, 106, 145

Galway City Council, 172, 181

Galway City Development Plan, 174, 177

Galway City Museum, 85, 93–4, 98, 106

Galway Education Centre, 92

Galway Film Fleadh, 106

Galway Hooker, 6

Galway–Mayo Institute of Technology (GMIT), 28, 93, 115

Galway Planning and Transportation Study, 174–5

Galway Port, 27

Galway Race Festival, 31, 107, 111–12, 135, 138, 144

Galway Sessions Festival, 31, 107

Galway Shopping Centre, 69

'Galway Tent', 138

Galway United, 113

Galwegians, 113

Gavin, Frankie, 117

gCopaleen, Myles na, 116

Gogarty, Oliver St. John, 2, 80
Great Famine, 55, 151
Gregory, Lady, 124
Greyhound Racing track, 114

Hall of the Red Earl, 20, 34, 98
Harbour Basin, 15–16
Hardiman, James, 6, 59, 139
Headford Road, 69–70, 168, 178, 190, 210, 213
Hewlett Packard, 28
Higgins, Michael D., 122–4
History of Galway, 6, 59, 139
Hy Brazil, 9

Inchigoill, 12
Inchiquin, 12

Jesuits, 27
Joyce, James, xvii, xix, 125

Keane, Dolores, 117
Keane, J.B., 86
Kennedy, John F., 126, 143, 144
'kicking the wall', 8
Kilkelly, H., 15
King Breasal, 9
Kirwans, 22

Leisureland, 8
Lennon, John, 6
Lock House, 36
Long Walk, 85, 98
Lough Atalia, 4, 12–13
Lough Corrib, 3, 4, 9–12, 14, 19, 40, 57, 59, 140, 165, 169, 203–4
Lough Mask, 9, 12
Lynch's Castle, 21, 48, 52, 83–4, 139, 222

Lynches, 21

Macken, Walter, 17, 125
Macnas, xviii, 106, 107, 110–11, 207
Parade, 31, 136
Martin, Richard, 116
Mayoralty House, 53, 85
McNeice, Louis, 143
McDonagh, Ringo, 117
McGowan, Shane, 6
Medtronic, 28
Mellow, Liam, 96
Menlo village, 57, 59–60, 66, 136, 204
Merit Medical, 28
Merlin Park Hospital, 56
Mervue United, 113
Meyrick Hotel, 29, 55, 87
Monroe's, 117
Morrison, Richard, 85
Mulvany, J.S., 87

National University of Ireland Galway (NUIG), 28, 86, 91, 103–5, 115, 142, 144
Nimmo, Alexander, 15
Nimmo's Pier, 55
Normans, 19–21, 48–50, 75
Nun's Island, 26, 38

O'Brien's Bridge, 211
O'Casey, Sean, 124
O'Conaire, Padraig, 96, 125
O'Connor, Martin, 117
O'Connor, Turlough, 19
O'Flahertys, 19
O'Hallorans, 19

O'Laoire, Murray, 93

Oranmore, 174, 176–7, 201, 223

Oyster Festival, 31, 107, 112–13

Pearse, Padraig, 144

Pearse Stadium, 113

pedestrianisation, 96, 118–20, 181, 211–3, 221

Persee family, 24, 124

Planning and Development Act (2000), 158

Planning Acts (1963), 62, 155

Poor Clare Convent, 26

Pope John Paul, 126

Public Transport Feasibility Study (2009), 182

Quincentennial Bridge, 180

Quincentennial Fountain, 96

Rahoon, 64, 66

Railway Hotel, *see* Meyrick Hotel

Reagan, Ronald, 126, 143

Renmore, 66, 202

Renmore and Its Environs, 66

Rain on the Wind, 17, 125

Red Earl Hall, *see* Hall of the Red Earl

Richard II, 20

Richard III, 21

'Riders to the Sea', 7

River Corrib, 3, 4, 8–12, 19, 33, 40, 49–50, 55, 57, 64, 75, 86, 97, 99, 101, 103, 140, 162, 168–9, 181, 203–5, 211, 213

River Shannon, 33

Riverfront 'Green' City, 203–6

Robinson, J.J., 88, 90

Roofhome City, 199–200

Salmon Weir Bridge, 10, 98, 100

Salthill, 6, 8, 29, 56, 102, 113, 163, 169–70, 202–3, 214–6

Salthill Devon, 113

Santiago de Compostela, 25

Saturday market, 128–30

Scott, Tallon, Walker, 91

Scott, William, 88

Seafront Railway City, 201–3

Shannon Airport, 29

Shannon, Sharon, 117

Shaw, George Bernard, 124

Shop Street, 70–1, 96–7

Spanish Arch, 16, 52, 75, 84–5, 93, 98, 143, 222

Spanish Armada, 7, 26, 142

St. Augustine, 13

St. Brendan the Navigator, 12

St. John, St. Oliver, 51

St. Mary's Diocesan College, 56, 88

St. Nicholas' Church, 25, 50, 52, 82–3, 106, 128, 144, 222

St. Patrick's Day Festival, 31, 110, 136

stone, 31–47

    cladding, 46

    construction, 40–2

    cut, 39, 45

    Galway, 37–8

    nature of, 34–6

    rubble, 39

    styles, 42–7

suburbia, 66, 152–4, 160–1, 223
sustainability, 158–62, 174, 176, 197, 204–5, 217–8
Synge, John Millington, 7, 124

Taafes, 117
Taibhdhearc Theatre, 125
Taylor's Hill, 26
Terryland Park, 113
Thackeray, W.M., 55
Thermo King, 28
Tigh Coili, 117
Tigh Neachtain, 107, 116, 117
tourism, 8, 29–31, 56, 63, 65, 134, 148, 164, 209
Tourist City, 209–11
Town Hall Theatre, 99, 106
traffic, 29, 66, 69, 75, 119, 145, 150, 164–6, 176, 178–84, 212–3, 215, 223, *see also* transport
transport, 8, 10, 29, 82, 153, 156, 159–61, 168, 178–87, 195, 197–8, 201–2
    public, 65–6, 144, 149–50, 154, 162, 176, 178, 181–93, 219, 223
'Tribes of Galway', 21, 136, 164

Tulca Visual Arts Festival, 31, 106
Turner, Richard, 87
Tyco, 28

UCHG Nurses Home and Hospital, 88–90
Ulysses, xix
urban design, 156, 190, 192, 194–6, 217, 223
Urban Renewal Act (1986), 62, 71

Vikings, 10, 18–20, 47
Volvo Ocean Race, 16, 112

'walking the prom', 8
walled town, 48–50, 75
Waterside, 99
Waterways area, 101–2
Wilde, Oscar, 12, 97
Wilde, William, 12
Williamite wars, 25, 27
Woodquay, 99, 213

Yeats, W.B., 111, 124